# THE TROPICAL GARDEN

New Edition *with 291 full-color illustrations*

*Text by* William Warren
*Photographs by* Luca Invernizzi Tettoni

Thames and Hudson

*© 1991 and 1997*
*Thames and Hudson Ltd, London*

*First published in the United States of America in 1991 by Thames and Hudson Inc., 500 Fifth Avenue, New York, New York 10110*
*New edition 1997*

*Library of Congress Catalog Card Number 96-60183*

*ISBN 0-500-01733-6*

*Printed and bound in Singapore*

# THE TROPICAL GARDEN

# Contents

# Introduction

FOR CENTURIES, LONG BEFORE it assumed any clearly defined shape, the alluring concept of a tropical garden was part of the European imagination. Eden was perhaps the earliest manifestation, that paradise of eternal bloom and fruitful abundance, whose loss seemed so painful to devout dreamers in the sands and snows of less hospitable climates; but there were doubtless other, more personal visions conjured up on dark winter nights, similar places where summer never ceased and nature yielded its marvels with little or no labour.

An element of reality entered such fantasies with the age of exploration, first through drawings and dried specimens brought back by adventurous botanists, later through some of the living plants, many of them every bit as bizarre as any of the vague imaginings. (The tropics hid no 'man-eating tree', as legend claimed, or at least none has been found; but in Borneo and the Philippines there were exceedingly odd pitcher plants that trapped and then slowly digested quite large insects.) Thanks to such revelations, painters could enhance their ideal gardens with increasingly accurate ferns and palms and exotic fruit trees – the banana often turned up as the tree of the knowledge of good and evil – even though the jungles in which they allegedly grew bore a remarkable resemblance to the neat, orderly arrangement of home.

The European fascination for tropical plants reached a peak during the 19th century, when scarcely any major capital, however frigid, lacked some sort of facility for displaying the latest botanic wonder to the public. Nowhere was this more evident than in England; moreover, odd though the suggestion may seem, it can also be argued that no country had a greater influence on the subsequent development of pleasure garden designs and their plant components far away in the actual tropics.

*Luxuriant, faintly mysterious, the tropical garden reflects many of man's oldest dreams with its never-ending growth and splashes of exotic colour.*

Strelitzia Reginae, *the Bird of Paradise flower; early drawings like this excited the European interest in tropical plants and led to both personal and official collections.* (Redouté les Liliacées, *v. 2, plate 78*).

As their empire spread, it became possible for the English to travel in comparative safety to the rain forests of Borneo and Malaya, to the lush islands of the West Indies, to Central America, India, Burma, and the South Pacific — to the native habitats, that is, of just about every tropical plant. (To give some idea of this wealth, Malaya alone offered some 8,000 species.) Given their long-established passion for horticulture back home, not to mention a growing demand from wealthy plant collectors and such celebrated botanic centers as Kew, it was not surprising that many of these wanderers sought to bring back a few specimens for both pleasure and profit.

Also unsurprisingly, their early efforts more often than not ended in disaster. Live plants usually died during the long sea

8

*F*ascinated
*Victorians view a new exotic
specimen at Kew (from* The
Illustrated London News, *17
October 1846).*

*D*rawing of a
*Wardian case for carrying plants
and seeds from exotic places, from
N. Ward,* Closed Cases for Plants
*(British Library).*

voyages of the time, and seeds were not that much more successful, either having lost their viability by the time they arrived or, if they were successfully germinated, soon withering in the hostile climate.

The 'greenhouse' or 'conservatory' — two words that originated in the 17th century — was an early effort to overcome this problem. The Orangery at Kew, built in 1761, was at first heated by hot-air flues, later by hot water. Temperatures were difficult to control in such structures, however, and the extensive use of glass to increase the tropical atmosphere was for a long time curtailed by both a lack of good-quality sheet glass and a prohibitive tax.

A major breakthrough took place in 1827 when a London physician named Nathaniel Ward, by way of experiment, placed a caterpillar in a glass jar with a bit of mould and then stoppered the jar. He apparently forgot about it, and when he inspected the jar later he found that a small fern and a blade of grass were growing out of the mould, nurtured by moisture that had condensed on the inside.

There is no record of what happened to the caterpillar — presumably the object of the original experiment — but the plants flourished for four years and the discovery gave birth to the famous Wardian case which, in the words of Tyler Whittle in his delightful book *The Plant Hunters*, 'so revolutionized the transport of exotics that plant hunting up to 1834 might appropriately be called pre-Wardian, and the intensive collecting done afterward, post-Wardian.'

Ward produced a large-sized version of his jar, consisting of glass panes supported by hard, seasoned wood. One result of this was a rage for what were called terraria, little indoor gardens that became a familiar item of Victorian interior decoration. Another, far more important, was a dramatic improvement in the survival rate of plants moved from one part of the world to another. Thanks to the so-called Wardian cases (from which, incidentally, the doctor derived no profits), delicate tropical specimens arrived safely in England and elsewhere from distant places, there to be proudly installed in huge, glass-covered gardens that were also fortuitously entering a period of mass popularity around the same time.

The development of these glasshouses was an outgrowth of the repeal of Britain's Glass Tax in 1845, together with the rise of new industries producing quality glass at far lower cost than ever before. Literally thousands of such structures appeared in England

*The great Palm House at Kew, built by Decimus Burton between 1844 and 1848 to display palms and other ornamental plants brought from the tropics (from* The Illustrated London News, *7 August 1852).*

– 'Tropic Squares' they were called by the Poet Laureate of the day – ranging from tiny outhouses in suburban backyards to Decimus Burton's splendid Palm House at Kew, constructed between 1844 and 1848 and covering 24,200 square feet; and wealthy collectors vied to see who could amass the greatest number of exotic plants for their own increasingly grand private glasshouses.

The sixth Duke of Devonshire, for instance, sent one of his gardeners, a young man named John Gibson, to India in 1835 with the particular mission of bringing back an *Amherstia nobilis*, reputed to be the most beautiful flowering tree in the world with its masses of coral-coloured blossoms. Despite acute suffering from the heat, which somehow came as a surprise, Gibson got his *Amherstia*,

*Joseph Paxton's*
*Great Conservatory at*
*Chatsworth, at its time the largest*
*glass-covered area in the world*
*(from the Devonshire Collection).*

along with a collection of other tropical specimens that filled thirteen of the then-new Wardian cases, and then raced back to England on the fastest possible ship. Joseph Paxton, the Duke's head gardener, had constructed a special glasshouse to receive the tender plants and was at the port to meet Gibson and speed the cases to Chatsworth by a relay team of coaches.

Paxton became the most famous of all glasshouse designers. His Great Conservatory at Chatsworth, built between 1836 and 1840, was the largest glass-covered area in the world, wide enough for Queen Victoria to ride through in her carriage. Another similar glasshouse on the estate enabled the Duke to enjoy the first English flowering of the huge Brazilian water lily, given the name

*Victoria Regia* in honour of the Queen (the name was later changed to *Victoria Amazonica*). Kew also built a special house for the *Victoria*, designed by Richard Turner and completed in 1852, and so did almost every major botanical garden in Europe; the platter-like leaves became as much a part of the popular tropical-garden image as the elegant Traveller's Palm and the giant-leafed *Alocasia*, or 'Elephant's Ear'.

Both the Wardian case and the great Victorian glass-houses played prominent roles in the development of ornamental landscapes in the tropics as we know them today. Economic gardens had been important to hot-weather colonial possessions since the early days of empire, mainly for experiments with plants of potential commercial value. The one at St Vincent in the West Indies was established in 1764 (Captain William Bligh was headed there in the *Bounty* with a cargo of young breadfruit trees when the famous mutiny broke out), and others followed in Jamaica (1774), Calcutta (1786), Penang (1796), Ceylon (1821), and Singapore (1822). Wardian cases greatly facilitated the task of bringing new specimens to these centres, not only such future money-earners as rubber, coffee, oil palm, and spices but countless ornamentals as well. This accelerated the dispersal that would eventually bring exotic plants from the jungles of Central America to gardens in Singapore, from the South Seas to Trinidad, many of them quickly becoming so acclimatized that within a few generations they were regarded as almost native species.

*The Great Conservatory at Chatsworth (top), where the sixth Duke of Devonshire kept his collection of tropical exotics.*

*A Victoria Regia flower, by J. F. Allen.*

*The Victoria Regia, (now Amazonica) water lily (bottom), in a glasshouse constructed especially for its cultivation by Joseph Paxton at Chatsworth.*

To cite but a few common examples, the Bougainvillea, Allamanda, Plumeria, Poinsettia, Heliconia, Anthurium, Bromeliad, and Philodendron — now standard garden plants throughout the tropical world — all originated in Central and South America, and most were introduced elsewhere during the past century.

The influence of the glasshouses was more subtle but no less significant. To understand it, one must remember that the concept of a private garden planted purely for aesthetic purposes was generally alien to tropical countries. Many royal palaces and religious buildings, it is true, had gardens, though more often than not these were rather formal and symbolic, with the choice of plants and sometimes even their location being determined by a number of mystical factors. In the highly developed urban centres of ancient India, wealthier families also planted extensive pleasure parks of trees and shrubs with fragrant flowers (particularly those mentioned in poetry) as well as artificial lakes and pools, often with fountains.

But there was no such tradition of ornamental horticulture among the inhabitants of most hot-weather places. Around the average home there might be a few specimens chosen especially because of their scented flowers or because they were believed to bring good fortune; the greatest number of plants, however, were strictly utilitarian, grown for their fruits or medicinal properties rather than for the pleasure of viewing their flowers or foliage. Nor would much, if any, attention be paid to attractive landscape design in such gardens: early accounts by travellers in the tropics abound in enthusiastic descriptions of jungle scenery, but a reader will search in vain for one praising the tasteful arrangement of massed ornamental beds and contrasting lawns of well-trimmed grass around the homes of natives.

These features were largely European contributions to the tropical garden and many of them were based on memories of effects seen in those glass-covered wonderlands back in England, Holland, and France with their tastefully arranged collections of ferns and lacy palms, their imaginative use of meandering pathways and man-made water features, above all, perhaps, their fondness for beds of colourful shrubs, chosen for either their flowers or leaf patterns, a 19th-century garden fashion both inside the glasshouses and out.

Such 'tame jungles', as one writer has called them, were generally first seen in the great botanical gardens like Buitenzorg

('Free of Care') at Bogor, which served as the official residence of the Governors-General of the Dutch East Indies, and Singapore, in which, from its beginning, large areas were designed for pleasant evening strolls and Sunday-afternoon band concerts. They were later emulated on a smaller scale in private compounds, initially those of colonial officials and later spreading to the more Westernized local upper classes.

The development was slower in the rare tropical countries that escaped colonization, of which Thailand is the only example in Southeast Asia. M.R. Pimsai Amranand, whose *Gardening in Bangkok* is the standard work on the subject, writes that when she returned from many years of study in England, 'My first impression of gardens in Bangkok was of flat pieces of land with spindly fruit trees planted all along the fences, with herbs and flowers planted in ugly raised beds completely straight, looking vaguely like graves . . . The emphasis was on the plants with little thought of how a garden should look or of making a garden. The word "suan" in Thai and translated as "garden" conjures up in Thai minds a place that the English would call an orchard or market garden.'

Today, a mere twenty years after her book was first published, Bangkok abounds in fine examples of what is generally perceived as 'the tropical garden' – that is, an artful blend of exotic plants and basically European concepts of landscape design, in many cases far more spacious than the glasshouse arrangements of the past but not unlike them in general effect.

This sort of modern tropical garden belongs to no particular place or culture, if indeed it ever did. With the advent of air travel, the dispersal of ornamentals has accelerated at such a rate that new plants are constantly being introduced, getting acclimatized, and turning into standards within an amazingly short time. When the Bali Hyatt Hotel opened in 1973, for instance, hundreds of trees, shrubs, and ground covers were used in its extensive gardens, many brought from nearby Singapore but others from as far as Hawaii and South America; today most of these can be found all over Bali, not only in gardens but growing wild in the jungles. Of more than 100 specimens photographed for a book published in 1977 on tropical exotics found in Hawaiian gardens, only one was native to Hawaii and the great majority were fairly late introductions, some so recent that the authors were able to name the collectors who had brought them to the islands.

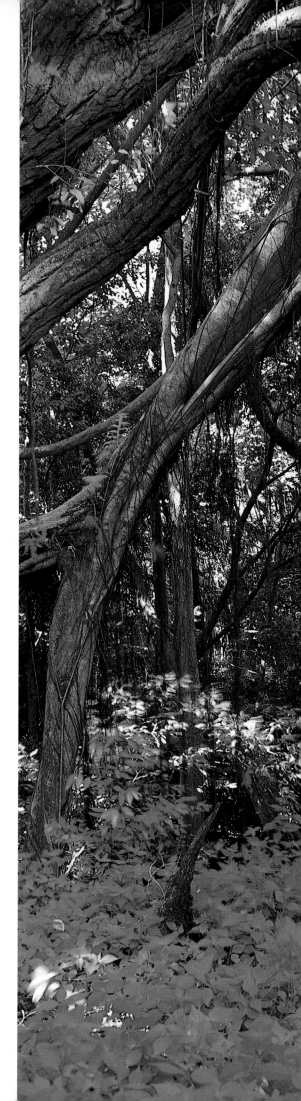

Given only the plant material to judge from, then, minus any revealing architectural features, it would be impossible to say whether most contemporary tropical gardens are located in Bali or Bangkok, Singapore or Miami, Honolulu or Kandy.

Moreover, the term 'tropical' can be misleading, particularly to a layman, suggesting a certain uniformity of conditions: constant heat, of course, plentiful rainfall, rich soil. In fact, conditions vary almost as much in the tropics as in temperate countries, not just from country to country but even within a single locale. Cibodas on Java is a tropical garden, but it is located at an elevation of nearly 2,000 metres and the weather is cool enough to support numerous temperate-zone plants as well. Thailand certainly qualifies as tropical in terms of temperature, but many parts of the country have almost no rain at all for nearly half the year and soil conditions are so diverse that a separate gardening book would be required for each region. Without leaving the residential suburbs of Honolulu, one can find an assortment of micro-climates ranging from wet to dry, from sea level to fairly high elevations, each quite different in the demands it makes on a horticulturist.

Given these differences, no work of the present sort, covering gardens in several parts of the tropical world, could hope to provide any very practical information on cultivation. Its purpose, rather, is to show some of the ways garden owners in the tropics have made creative use of their varied landscapes, climates, and plant material. Gardeners elsewhere might find useful inspiration through certain features – a pleasing pathway, an unusual fountain, an interesting combination of colours or leaf textures, even the plants themselves (many of which can be grown far from their tropical homelands) – or they might merely discover new images which which to adorn the ancient, ever-compelling dream of paradise.

*A* grove of Ficus
*trees spread their dramatic aerial*
*roots along a road in Hawaii.*

16

# Religious and Royal Gardens

*A reclining Buddha image under a Bodhi tree (*Ficus religiosa*) near the old Thai capital of Ayutthaya.*

*A pond in a Thai Buddhist temple at Petchburi serves an aesthetic as well as a practical function. The building on the right is a library, built over the water to protect manuscripts from white ants.*

*T*he earliest gardens of the tropics were those planted in the compounds of religious complexes and around the palaces of local royalty. A simple desire for beautiful surroundings was seldom the sole motive in creating these landscapes. Symbolism and tradition were often equally important factors, not only in architectural and decorative features but also in the selection of plants to be included and their precise locations. Nevertheless, within their various cultures, such gardens helped set aesthetic standards which in sometimes subtle ways can be detected in many contemporary designs.

*The Siwalai Garden (opposite), created as a recreation park for royal ladies who lived in the inner area of Bangkok's Grand Palace.*

*A traditional temple garden with a lotus pond, as shown in a mural painting at Bangkok's Wat Mongkut.*

*A Thai ceremonial offering; the food container is made of banana leaves, while the flowers are lotus blooms with the petals folded back and jasmine buds attached by hand to a branch to resemble a blossoming spray.*

IT IS DIFFICULT, IF NOT IMPOSSIBLE, to accurately reproduce the original gardens of most tropical palaces and religious complexes. None has been preserved unchanged over the centuries: in some cases, the architectural concept remains but new plants have been introduced and entirely different (often European-inspired) landscape designs have been superimposed, while in others the buildings have vanished altogether and the only sources are vague descriptions in official chronicles. Yet there were certainly gardens, often quite beautiful ones, and they were undoubtedly the earliest to be planted in the tropics; moreover, even from the scant evidence at hand it is possible to make a few general comments on their design and components.

Not surprisingly, given the climate, water was an important element, in religious compounds as well as royal pleasure gardens. Hindu, Buddhist, and Chinese temples all incorporated ponds, pools, fountains, and often extensive artificial lakes in their landscapes, either for ritual bathing or merely decoration and a cooling effect. In many cases – the Hindu temples of Bali, for example – such water features displayed complex engineering skills, involving aqueducts and ornamental fountains, and formed an integral part of the architectural concept. In others, designs of pools reflected familiar emblems of the religion; a famous one at Anuradhapura, the ancient capital of Sri Lanka, is in

*A* Bodhi tree growing on one of the terraces of the Shwedagon Pagoda in Rangoon.

*S*tone figure used as a fountain at Goa Gajah, the 'Elephant Cave', an 11th-century religious site in Bali.

*T*he Lotus Pool at Anuradhapura, ancient capital of Sri Lanka.

*Tirta Empul, one of the most sacred places in Bali, dating from the 10th century; the spring from which the water comes is known as 'the Fountain of Immortality'. By regarding places of unusual beauty as holy and re-landscaping them in the form of gardens, the Balinese have succeeded in preserving the environment and creating what is possibly the most beautiful island on earth.*

the shape of a huge lotus blossom, the petals serving as steps to the deepest part.

Symbolism played an important role in the choice of plants for such gardens, with special prominence given to trees and shrubs that had acquired some sort of spiritual significance. The most important of these throughout tropical Asia were various species of Ficus, particularly *Ficus religiosa*, the so-called Bodhi tree, under which the Buddha is believed to have attained enlightenment. Buddhists, however, are not alone in attributing mystical qualities to Ficus trees; perhaps because of their spectacular aerial roots, which often form strange, twisted patterns and mysterious grottos, they have long been seen as an obvious abode for supernatural powers and thus also venerated by Hindus as well as by countless animistic groups.

In temple gardens, both modern and ancient, a large Ficus is nearly always given a special enclosure of its own, with some sort of shrine or altar nearby where offerings can be made. The tree is carefully tended, specialists being called in when disease strikes and the branches of an ageing specimen supported by poles to keep them from breaking; one at Anuradhapura is supposedly the oldest historical tree in the world, having been brought from India as a seedling in 288 BC and its life recorded ever since.

Of almost equal significance is *Nelumbo nucifera*, the lotus, which has acquired a wide-ranging collection of symbolic connotations, including fertility, prosperity, perfection, and the transitory nature of human existence. The lotus thrives in both tropical and temperate climates and is found in religious compounds from India to Japan, growing in lakes, moats, ornamental pools and large jars, as well as depicted in mural paintings, stone and wood carvings, ceramic designs, and architectural details.

24

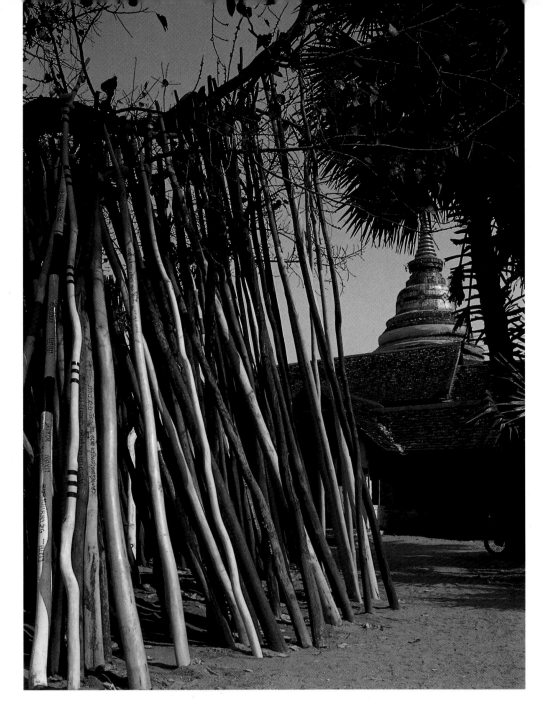

*Left: the poles around a venerable Bodhi tree at Wat Phra That Lampang Luang in northern Thailand are both offerings to the sacred tree and also supports to keep its branches from breaking.*

*Balinese offerings, collectively known as* banten, *come in a vast variety of shapes, colours, and materials, as those shown on this and the facing page suggest. In many, symbolism plays a part in both the colour and the number of flowers used and also in the shape of the offering. The* banten *at the bottom of this page, called* jejaitan, *are made of cut, plaited, and pinned palm leaves.*

25

*Plants figure prominently in classical Balinese paintings, as in these from the Kerta Gosa Hall of Justice, part of the palace at Klungkung.*

A more decorative tree than the Ficus is the Plumeria, popularly called Frangipani, a native of tropical America which has been cultivated in Asia for at least two centuries; in India it is sometimes known as the 'Temple tree' and is planted in Muslim cemeteries as well as Buddhist monastery gardens. Perhaps because of these associations, the tree was once considered unsuitable for private gardens in some places, though this aversion does not seem to have been very strong. (In Thailand, it was based more on linguistic than religious grounds; the local name, *lamtom*, sounds like *ra-tom*, the Thai word for 'sorrow', and thus the tree was thought to bring unhappiness.)

Saracas, natives of Southeast Asia from Malaysia to India, were used in many religious gardens for shade and for the beauty of their displays of yellow, orange, or red flowers, and so were various species of Brownea, which have large red or pink flower heads. A number of scented shrubs and creepers – Jasmine, for instance, and *Michelia alba* – were also popular, partly because of their fragrance and partly because they provided a ready source of flowers for the garlands presented in large quantities as offerings.

Water features were a prominent part of royal compounds as well. The Taman Sari, also known as the 'Water Castle' and used for recreation by the Sultans of Yogyakarta in Java, was an ingenious aquatic pleasure palace, surrounded by a broad moat and containing innumerable canals, conduits, ponds, and intimate private bathing pools. At Klungkung on the island of Bali, the Puri Smarapura ('Palace of the God of Love') had a graceful pavilion with painted ceilings in the centre of a lake, fed by water that spurted from the mouths of stone animals, while at Tirtagangga – literally, though not accurately, 'Ganges Water' – there is an extensive network of once-royal ponds and fountains, now a popular bathing spot for local children.

Plants, too, were often similar, with the notable exception of *Ficus religiosa*. Flowering trees and shrubs with scented flowers were popular, especially those frequently mentioned in poetry like *Saraca indica*, *Michelia alba*, and Jasmine, and many gardens also contained specimens used in cooking, traditional medicines, and making the complex floral offerings that were often a speciality of palace women. Symbolism, however, still played a significant role: at the Kraton (Royal Palace) of Yogyakarta, the choice and exact siting of plants was determined by a complex (and, to an outsider, somewhat obscure) pattern based

*The bathing pools at Tirtagangga – literally, 'Ganges Water' – part of a former palace in Bali and now popular with local children (opposite).*

27

*P*art of the
*Siwalai Garden in Bangkok's*
*Grand Palace; Ixora are among*
*the clipped shrubs that line the*
*pathways of this private garden,*
*reserved for the royal family.*

on their local names, which in turn suggested such concepts as 'hopeful', 'youth', and 'mutual understanding'.

More subject to changing fashions than religious compounds, palace landscapes were the first to respond to Western innovations and today few, if any, exist in their original form. A notable example is the Siwalai Garden of Bangkok's Grand Palace, intended as a recreation area for the sizeable population of royal wives and children who lived in an adjacent walled section which even today, long after the last resident has departed, is closed to most outsiders. The palace was constructed between 1782 and 1785 as a replica of one in the former capital of Ayutthaya, and both it and the garden were extensively altered over the next century or so.

29

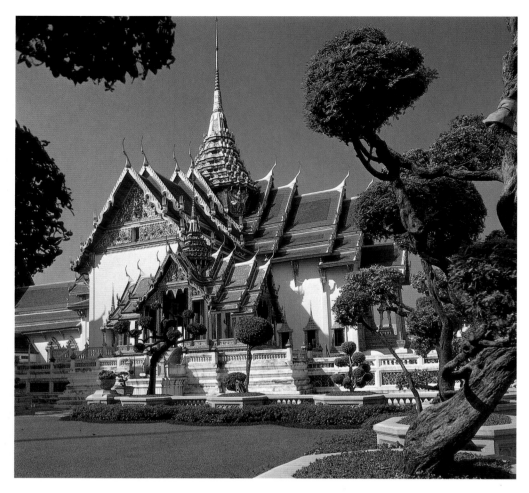

Under the Bangkok dynasty's second king, for example, the Siwalai Garden was dominated by a large lake containing several islands; on these there were Chinese-style pavilions and a small theatre where classical Thai dramas were performed. The third king, a pious Buddhist, disapproved of such frivolity and dismantled most of the garden, though retaining some of the Chinese statuary which adorned it. King Rama IV partially restored the area and added a personal chapel in traditional Thai style faced with grey marble.

The garden that remains today was essentially laid out in the fifth reign – a rectangular expanse flanked at one end by the Western-style Baromphiman Mansion and at the other by a classic Thai structure built in 1879 to house statues of past kings, with King Rama IV's chapel in the middle. Numerous Plumeria trees are planted in the lawns, and pathways are lined with fragrant shrubs, often clipped in the geometric shapes popular in both royal and religious Thai gardens. Chinese influence, strong during much of the 19th century, is evident in stone figures used as decorations and in two moon gates leading through one wall into the former women's quarter.

*Stately Royal Palms (*Roystonea*) tower in the Siwalai Garden; the Chinese figures on the lawn below became popular garden ornaments during the early 19th century when many came to Thailand as ballast on ships returning from the rice trade.*

30

Elsewhere in Bangkok is another royal garden surrounding the all-teakwood Vimarn Mek Palace, built in 1900 by King Rama V and restored by Her Majesty Queen Sirikit in 1982 as part of the dynasty's bicentennial celebration. The present planting is a blend of original trees and newer ornamentals – mostly shrubs and annuals – added during the restoration. The tallest trees in the compound belong to the Dipterocarpus family, indigenous to Thailand and a source of much-valued hard wood for furniture. *Vatica scortechini* and *Ochrocarpus siamensis*, also native trees, are planted close to the palace; both have small but fragrant flowers and the latter is also used in traditional Thai medicine. A number of fruit trees like Mango, Tamarind, Custard Apple, and Jackfruit further reflect the old Thai philosophy that even royal landscapes should be practical as well as aesthetically appealing.

*Part of the garden at Vimarn Mek Palace; most of this area was re-landscaped during restoration of the palace in 1982.*

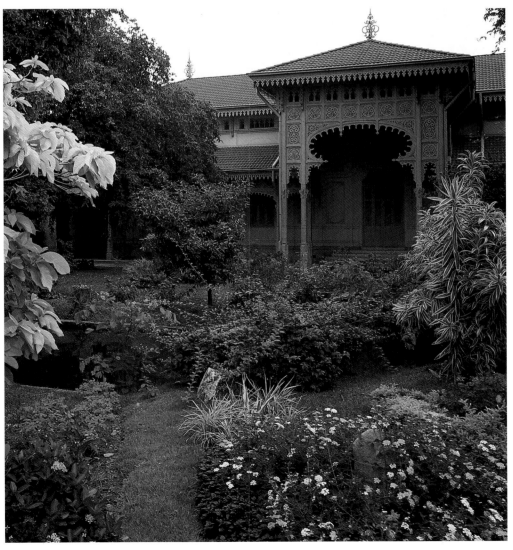

*A* European
statue in a covered pavilion at the
entrance to Vimarn Mek.

*S*hrubs selected
for their flowers and colourful
foliage, near one of the auxiliary
buildings in the palace gardens.

# Botanical Gardens

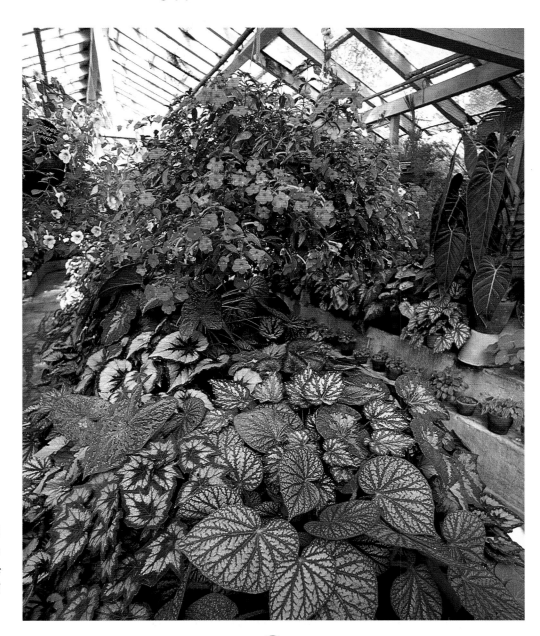

*A massed display of Begonias and other ornamental plants in a glasshouse at Sri Lanka's famous Peradeniya Botanical Garden.*

*Ornamentals from various parts of the world have been introduced into a rich natural environment at the Lyon Arboretum in Hawaii.*

*Originally created as centres of scientific research where potential commercial crops could be tested, the great tropical botanical gardens also played a major role in the dispersal of ornamental plants throughout the world and, in some cases, have produced hybrids that later became popular standards. Moreover, most were designed to provide aesthetic pleasure as well as to serve as a showcase for collections, and their often European landscape features – artificial lakes and sweeping lawns, atmospheric pathways and massed beds of exotic specimens – provided a powerful inspiration to private gardeners.*

*A memorial built by Thomas Stamford Raffles to his wife Olivia, who died at Bogor during Raffles' brief tenure as Governor of Java.*

*An avenue of Canarium trees at the Kebun Raya, festooned with assorted creepers and epiphytic plants; one 19th-century visitor called this 'the finest avenue of trees in the world'.*

THE FIRST BOTANICAL GARDEN in the tropics was Pamplemousses, established on the Indian Ocean island of Mauritius in 1735. Over the next century, numerous others followed as European countries acquired more and more colonial possessions, eventually forming a horticultural network that stretched around the world from the West Indies to Southeast Asia.

Nearly all such gardens were originally economic, places for testing various new crops that might be grown commercially, and in this effort they were dramatically successful; Pamplemousses, for example, helped develop the vital sugar industry of Mauritius, and the Singapore Botanical Garden was responsible for introducing rubber to Malaya. At the same time, they also acclimatized countless ornamental specimens brought from distant places, and since most such gardens served a recreational as well as a scientific purpose they exerted a powerful influence on the development of modern tropical garden designs.

One of the oldest and most celebrated of Asia's botanical gardens is the Kebun Raya at Bogor in Java. Though located at an altitude of only 260 metres on the slope of Mount Salak, Bogor enjoys much cooler weather than the capital of Jakarta, some 54 kilometres to the north, and this is what led the Dutch Governor-General Baron Gustaaf von Imhoff to build a summer house there in 1744. He called it Buitenzorg ('Free of Care'), and it continued to be known by this name for the remaining two centuries of Dutch rule, during which the Baron's house was replaced by a much grander, white-columned structure that from 1870 to 1942 served as the residence of Governors-General of the Dutch East Indies.

It was not the Dutch, however, who originally conceived the idea of planting a botanical garden around Buitenzorg. As one of the complex international results of the Napoleonic Wars, the British briefly occupied Java and from 1811 to 1816 their representative was Thomas Stamford Raffles, later to achieve fame as the founder of Singapore. A keen amateur botanist, Raffles was also a strong believer in the value of 'economic gardens' and saw that Bogor was an ideal site for one with its rich volcanic soil and plentiful rainfall. He is sometimes also credited with laying out the design of the Kebun Raya, but this was in fact done by Professor C.G.L. Reinwardt and two assistants from Kew, in England; the garden was officially opened in 1817, the year after Raffles left.

*T*ree ferns and *Birds' Nest Ferns thrive in the cool air of Cibodas, a high-elevation extension of the Kebun Raya garden.*

38

*Epiphytes grow on the gnarled trunks of century-old trees at Bogor.*

*Victoria Amazonica water lilies in a pond at the Kebun Raya garden.*

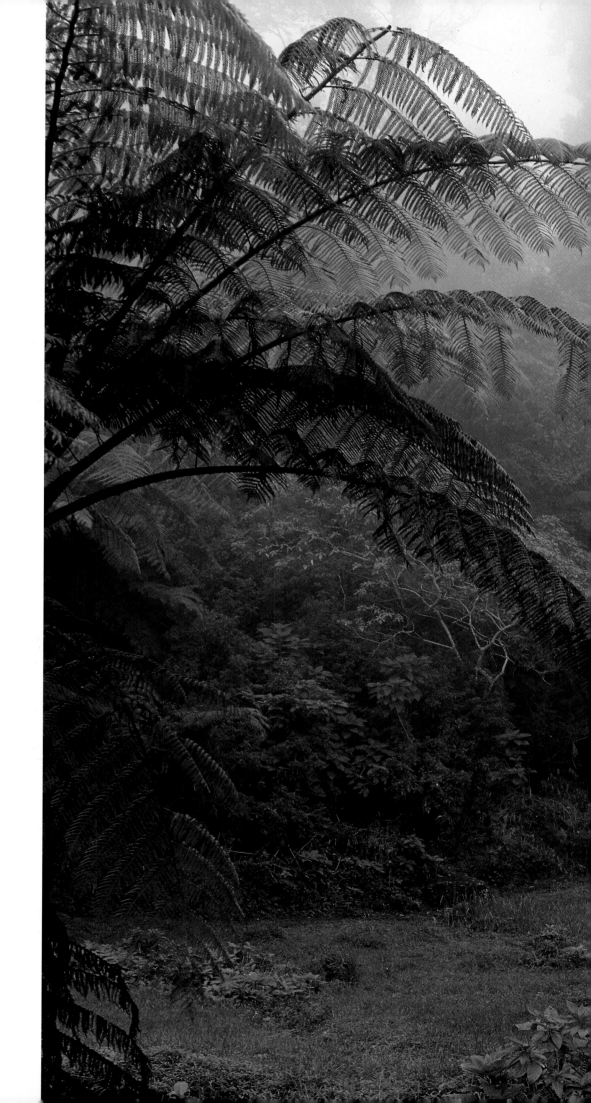

*T*ree ferns
(Cyathea) *in one of the misty
valleys at Cibodas, a garden with
unusually high rainfall at an
elevation of nearly 2,000 metres.*

When the Dutch returned, they so improved and expanded the Kebun Raya that by the end of the century it was known as one of the world's foremost tropical plant collections. Important research was done on such commercial crops as tea, cassava, tobacco, oil palm, and chichona (quinine), all of which contributed to Indonesia's wealth. In addition, surrounding the palace as it did, the garden became equally famous as an imaginatively landscaped pleasure park for members of the colonial élite who maintained homes nearby.

Particularly dramatic was its main drive lined with towering Canarium trees – 'the finest avenue of trees in the world', one visitor called it – each trunk covered with a tangled mass of staghorn and birds' nest ferns, Philodendrons (one of the many ornamentals introduced to Southeast Asia at Bogor), and epiphytic orchids, among them the giant Grammatophyllum, which has as many as 3,000 flowers at one blooming. Sweeping lawns were laid out, too, both around the palace and elsewhere in the garden, and the massed beds then so popular in Europe were planted with a wide assortment of exotic specimens to provide both flowers and colourful foliage.

The Kebun Raya today contains an estimated 15,000 species of trees and plants, as well as over 5,000 orchid varieties. One part of the 200-acre site has been left in its original rain-forest condition, while others are devoted to special collections, such as

*An English-style landscape in the Penang Botanical Garden.*

*Flower of a Cycad in Honolulu's Foster Botanical Garden (opposite top).*

*Amherstia nobilis, regarded by many as the most beautiful flowering tree (centre).*

*Flowers of the Cannonball tree (bottom).*

*Seeds growing out of the trunk of the so-called Cannonball Tree (far left).*

ferns, cacti, medicinal plants, palms, and bamboos. The best-maintained areas are those surrounding the palace, where tame deer (originally introduced by the Dutch as a source of venison) graze the lawns, and an extensive recreational section along both sides of Queen Astrid Avenue, where there are beds of multi-coloured Cannas and such ornamental trees as *Amherstia nobilis*, a native of Burma often called the most beautiful flowering tree in the world.

Above Bogor, at an elevation of nearly 2,000 metres, is Cibodas, an extension of the Kebun Raya established by the Dutch in 1889 for experiments with specimens that prefer cooler weather. This is decidedly European in design and atmosphere, with vast sloping lawns and numerous trees and shrubs more associated with temperate zones than with the tropics, collected from as far as South Africa and Australia. Thanks to an exceptionally high rainfall, Cibodas is rich in ferns and among its more striking features are valleys filled with lofty Tree Ferns and numerous smaller varieties.

43

*H*ouses of garden caretakers at Pamplemousses.

*A lily pond at Pamplemousses, the first botanical garden established in the tropics.*

*Part of the large collection of palms planted at Pamplemousses.*

At the pioneering Pamplemousses, what had begun mainly as a search for plants that might benefit colonial treasuries led eventually to the creation of a beautiful landscape; and this process was repeated elsewhere in the tropical world.

Sri Lanka also offered perfect conditions for a botanical garden. The idea was first raised by Sir Joseph Banks, Director of Kew, when the British took over the island in the early 19th century and the first efforts were made near Colombo. In 1821, however, the garden was moved to the royal capital of Kandy and there, known as Peradeniya, it became one of the showplaces of the East, renowned not only for its success with economic crops (it helped develop the Assam tea that is today Sri Lanka's principal export) but also for the beauty of its ornamental lawns and tree-lined walkways. (Over the objections of some of his associates, Lord Louis Mountbatten located his wartime headquarters in the gardens, calling it 'probably the most beautiful place in the world and a delightful place in which to work'.)

*One of the several lakes in the Singapore Botanical Garden, where carefully labelled plants from all over the tropics are displayed.*

*A jungle-like planting in the Botanical Garden; Pandanus pygmaeus, a dwarf variegated form, is seen in the foreground; in the background can be seen the spreading leaves of the Traveller's Palm (Ravenala madagascariensis)*

Singapore, like Bogor, owes its famous garden to Thomas Stamford Raffles, who planted a park of nutmeg, clove, and ornamental shrubs on Government Hill soon after his arrival in 1819. This first effort later foundered, but in 1859 a new, more spacious garden, designed principally for pleasure, was started by a private group called the Agri-Horticultural Society in the Tanglin District. Scenic roads and pathways were laid out, an artificial lake was excavated, and on a slight elevation, terraced and planted with flower beds, a regimental band began giving Sunday-afternoon concerts. Eventually, the Society's debts exceeded its income; in 1875 the garden was turned over to the government and finally became the botanical research centre Raffles had envisaged.

47

*Opposite: vines and other ornamental creepers are grown over trellises around this formal courtyard at the Singapore Botanical Garden.*

*The Bandstand, one of the oldest landmarks in the Singapore garden.*

*A gazebo at the entrance to the garden's jungle, where mostly indigenous plants grow.*

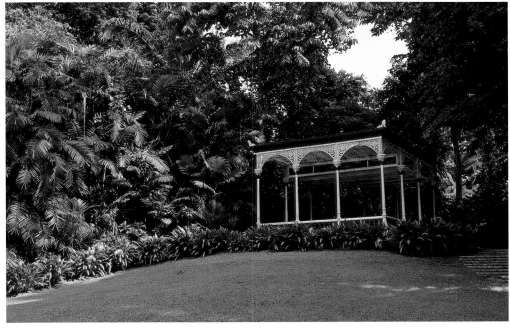

Its most celebrated commercial achievement was the introduction of rubber as a viable crop in Malaya, credit for which largely goes to a single-minded Director named Henry Nicholas Ridley, who discovered an innovative way of tapping the trees and earned the sobriquet of 'Mad Ridley' because of his fervent campaign to persuade planters to try *Hevea brasiliensis* instead of coffee. (The specimens he worked with were descendants of only eleven seedlings which reached Singapore in Wardian cases in 1877, having been germinated at Kew from Brazilian seeds.)

*Cordylines,*
*known in Hawaii as Ti plants,*
*are collected in this part of the*
*Lyon Arboretum, where their*
*varied foliage provides a*
*dramatic splash of colour. The*
*leaves are exported in*
*considerable quantities for use in*
*flower arrangements.*

*Overleaf*
*(p. 52–53): part of the garden at*
*the Lyon Arboretum; the*
*variegated leaves on the right*
*belong to a dwarf species of Ficus.*

While Ridley and others were changing the economy of the region, however, the Singapore garden remained the recreational centre planned by its founders, and countless new ornamental trees and shrubs, as well as orchid hybrids, were introduced there. It continued to function even during the Japanese occupation – two English botanists were allowed to stay out of prison camp to go on with their work – and, since the colony's independence, has been responsible not only for maintaining the original 84-acre site but also for implementing former Prime Minister Lee Kuan Yew's ambitious scheme to transform Singapore into a 'Garden City' with imaginative street plantings and public parks.

Another garden established by the British in the area was on the island of Penang in Malaya. Known as the Waterfall Gardens, this was planted in 1884, and while it never achieved the renown of Singapore as a centre of research it continues to be a popular recreational park.

Hawaii, America's tropical possession, also acquired a number of noted plant collections. As one botanist has written, 'every flower and plant we see in Hawaii is a traveller or the descendant of a traveller', since the islands originally rose from the sea as boiling masses of lava (a process that still continues) and whatever grows on them had to be brought in by one means or another. The earliest human settlers came from Polynesia, bringing such practical plants as the coconut, breadfruit, bamboo, and banana. Ornamentals arrived later, the great majority brought from all over the tropical world by local gardeners.

Reflecting this tradition of individual collecting, a number of Hawaii's best botanical gardens today began as private estates and retain many of their original landscape features. The Foster Botanic Garden, for example, now in downtown Honolulu, was started by a German doctor in the mid-19th century. He sold the property to Captain and Mrs Thomas Foster in 1867 and it was bequeathed to the city in 1930. Today, covering 20 acres, it is part of the Honolulu Botanic Gardens, which includes two other collections on the island of Oahu as well.

For 27 years, the director of the Foster Garden was Dr Harold Lyon, a noted orchid specialist who is also credited with introducing more than 10,000 ornamental trees and plants to Hawaii. The Lyon Arboretum at Manoa, now under the University of Hawaii, is a living monument to his horticultural achievements and contains an impressive collection of exotics in a setting that

encompasses dense, jungled valleys, exposed areas, and a variety of elevations. Though roughly divided into areas that highlight certain species – Cordylines, Gingers, Heliconias, Bromeliads, Aroids, ferns and the like – the Arboretum has been imaginatively landscaped to demonstrate the use of such plants for ornamental purposes.

*A variety of Costus, native to Central and South America.*

54

*Bromeliads in flower at the Lyon Arboretum.*

*A jungle-like pathway at the Lyon Arboretum, where various ornamentals are grown along with the original* forest cover; a Medinilla magnifica *blooms on the upper right, while below is a planting of* Impatiens.

# Colonial Style

*A house in Goa with a Mediterranean flavour, enhanced by a bright Bougainvillea; the window panes are made of seashells.*

*An old house from the colonial period on Mount Faber in Singapore, its spacious, park-like garden shaded by large trees.*

*B*oth urban areas and private gardens planted by Europeans who settled in various colonial possessions drew their inspirations from the remembered landscapes of home, particularly in the use of neatly clipped lawns and tree-lined drives. Even fast-growing, often unruly tropical shrubs and creepers achieved a sense of visual order when arranged in familiar beds and herbaceous borders. The influence of these arrangements on contemporary gardens was considerable and extended to a number of hot-weather countries – Thailand, for example – which had never undergone the colonial experience.

EARLY EUROPEANS WHO CAME to the tropics had conflicting emotions about their environment. The more romantic were entranced by the splendid luxuriance that surrounded them and responded like Isabella Bird, who travelled through Malaya in 1883: 'Vegetation rich, profuse, endless, rapid, smothering, in all shades of vivid green, from the pea-green of spring and the dark velvety green of endless summer to the yellow-green of the plumage of the palm.' Others, probably the majority of those who actually took up residence in such places, found it vaguely threatening: undisciplined and somehow suggestive of a moral laxity. They wanted a more controlled landscape, in part to conjure up nostalgic memories of home but also symbolically to repel the riotous jungle (and possibly riotous natives) that loomed on all sides.

And so, for the most part, they tried to reproduce Dutch cities in Java, British ones in Burma, Malaya, and the West Indies, French ones in Indo-China, Spanish ones in the Philippines. 'On each side of these Canals', wrote a visitor to Batavia (now Jakarta) in 1817, 'are planted Rows of fine Trees, that are always green, which, with the Beauty and Regularity of the Buildings, make the Streets look very agreeable; so that I think this City (for the bigness) one of the neatest and most beautiful in the whole World.' Other travellers admired similar evidence of orderly rule in Singapore, Rangoon, Saigon, and Manila and deplored the lack of it in non-colonial capitals like Bangkok, which did not acquire its first proper, Western-style street until the mid-19th century (and then only because foreign residents complained to the king that their health was suffering for lack of a place to take an evening carriage ride).

As Victor Savage comments in *Western Expressions of Nature and Landscape in Southeast Asia*, 'Such cities showed how Western taste had impregnated itself on the landscape. Here was a landscape neither natural nor indigenous, but fashioned according to the dictates of Western culture, technology, and aesthetic taste

*Veranda of the Presidential Palace at Bogor, overlooking the botanical gardens; the residence was built by the Dutch in the latter part of the 19th century.*

59

... The grid street patterns, canals, avenues and alleys, gardens, the geometrical flower beds and generally the spatial system of the Southeast Asian colonial cities were not only beautiful to many Western travellers, they were also emblems of security and comfort, and signs of dignified culture and civilization.'

What was true of the cities was equally true of the private gardens planted around the spacious bungalows and Victorian mansions of early settlers. The pride of most was its lawn, that ultimate reflection of horticultural order, laboriously weeded and clipped by native gardeners – small armies of them in the case of the really great lawns like those surrounding the residences of higher government officials. Reproduced, too, were the neat flower beds and herbaceous borders of home, also kept sternly under control through constant care. In many places Westerners tried to increase the illusion through imported seeds and bulbs. 'Great efforts were made to grow English flowers,' a former memsahib was

*Originally* introduced as a source of venison by the Dutch, deer still graze the lawns of the Presidential Palace at Bogor in Indonesia.

*Opposite: views* of the garden of the Presidential Palace at Bogor, which the Dutch called Buitenzorg, 'Free of Care'. The statues were added by President Sukarno.

*Victoria* Amazonica *in the reflecting lake at the entrance to the Presidential Palace.*

60

quoted as saying in *Plain Tales from the Raj*, 'which generally looked rather sickly in the Indian climate. We could have had the most marvellous gardens with orchids and all sorts of things, but no, they must be English flowers.' Later, as the choice of tropical specimens was increased through the work of botanical gardens, more adventurous plantings appeared that achieved familar effects with quite different materials and to more lasting effect.

If relatively few of these colonial gardens achieved real distinction, the main reason was perhaps that, more often than not,

*Shortage of labour was never a problem in the maintenance of European features in large colonial gardens; here a team of workers is shown rolling a lawn at the Gymkhana Club in Bombay.*

*A summer palace in the cool highlands of Java, near Cipanas; built by the Dutch around 1750, it was also a favourite retreat for Indonesia's President Sukarno.*

the houses belonged to the government or to business firms and the occupants changed regularly through transfer and retirement; whereas one might make serious efforts at planting an imaginative landscape, his successor might consider the continual upkeep too burdensome and prefer to settle for just a lawn, some shade trees, and perhaps a few beds of cheerfully bright Cannas and Hibiscus to offset the prevalent, eternal green.

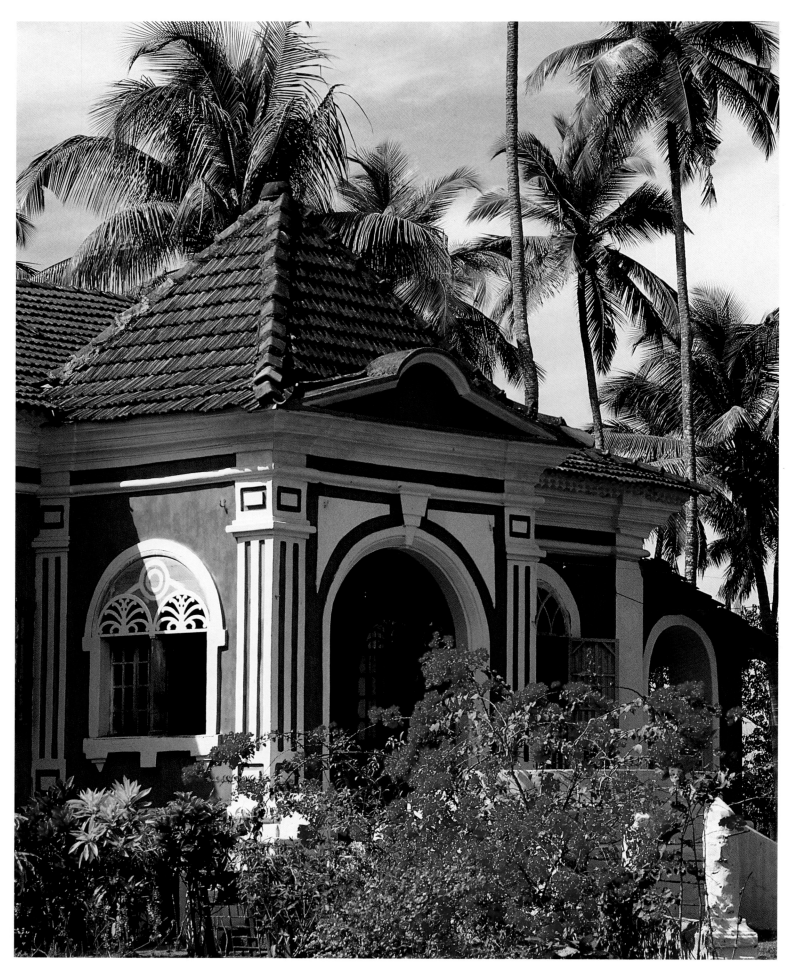

*A house from the colonial period in Penang; the flowers are* Delonix regia.

*A mansion at Chandor in Goa, now a museum.*

*A Chinese mansion in Phuket, Thailand; Caladiums grow in the foreground.*

*Opposite: an old mansion at Vagator, a small town on the sea in Goa; the bright colours of the house echo those of the Bougainvillea and shrubs in the garden.*

*The former House of Justice in Jakarta, completed in 1870; it now serves as the Museum of Fine Arts.*

There were important exceptions, however, particularly the gardens of the grander official residences like Buitenzorg in Bogor, where the Governors-General of the Dutch East Indies lived. Aside from a need to display its symbolic status, Buitenzorg could draw upon the immense resources of the adjacent botanical garden, not only for a ready supply of new and interesting plants but also for experienced landscape designers who laid out an overall plan that is still impressive a century later. Drives were lined with flowering trees from throughout the tropical world and two artificial lakes were excavated — the one in front rather formal and Western, reflecting the elegant white-columned residence and planted with the huge Brazilian *Victoria Amazonica* water lilies

*Bignonia ignea, the 'Flaming Trumpet Vine', blooms in the garden of an old bungalow in Chiang Mai, Thailand.*

that were all the rage in 19th-century Europe, and the one behind more irregular and natural, with a densely jungled island that served as a bird sanctuary.

The blend of apparently wild and meticulously maintained areas that one sees at the Bogor palace today was a reflection of the European movement away from rigidly formal plantings towards those that more closely approximated the random arrangements of nature. Tropical countries, of course, provided ideal opportunities for creating such landscapes, for nothing could be wilder looking than a patch of jungle, real or simulated, with its twisting vines and lush ferns, especially when it was contrasted with a trim lawn; and the best of the colonial gardens, both private and public, achieved this effect. In doing so, they forever altered local aesthetic concepts and led directly to the gardens of today.

67

# The Contemporary Tropical Garden

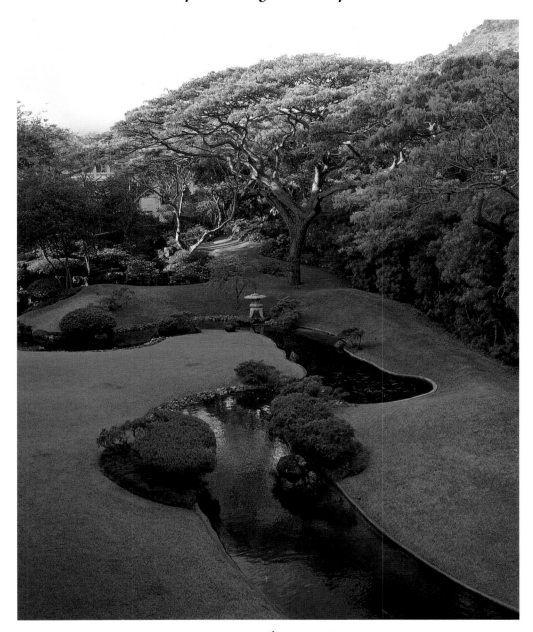

*A Japanese-style garden using tropical plants on the University of Hawaii campus, sheltered by large Rain Trees.*

*A private garden near Cibodas, in the highlands of Java, where Tree Ferns grow along with temperate-zone conifers.*

*A*t its best, the contemporary tropical garden is an artful blend of contrasting effects: of wild-looking areas and others meticulously maintained, of sun and shade, of artificial and natural features. While it might emulate familiar temperate-garden features – the well-trimmed lawn, the clipped hedge, the mixed bed – it cannot aspire to a slowly maturing but essentially unchanging design. It must be planned for continual growth and constantly altering vistas, thus presenting a challenge to gardeners while also offering the boon of seeing their dreams realized within the span of a very few years.

# The Mandai Gardens

JOHN AND AMY EDE have played an active role in Singapore gardening circles for more than forty years, introducing many plants to the island through their Mandai Gardens and also working with the Singapore Gardening Society, of which John Ede served as president for fourteen years.

Though the Mandai Gardens is primarily a commercial concern, specializing in orchids for export, one part has been landscaped to show how tropical plants can be employed in a garden. This consists of several areas both open and shady, with ponds, streams, and walkways along which ornamentals from all over the world can be seen. Heliconias, mainly from Central America, have been a particular interest of the Edes and they now have several dozen varieties ranging from dwarfs to gigantic stands several metres tall. These, together with such Alpinias as the so-called Red Ginger and a variety with bright yellow and green striped leaves, do well in Singapore's damp climate, where prolonged dry spells are rare.

The Mandai Gardens are also noted for their Mussaenda, especially a pink-flowering variety from the Philippines, as well as numerous unusual Dracaena, Calathea, and Cordylines, all of which bring year-round colour to a tropical garden with their splendidly patterned leaves.

*Densely planted beds are separated by well-trimmed lawns to create a sense of size in what is actually a relatively small area. On the right, Mussaenda, a native of the Philippines, provides an almost continual show of flowers against a background of Chrysalidocarpus palms.*

*Overleaf (pp. 72–73): dominating one part of the garden is a showy Traveler's Palm (Ravenala madagascariensis), actually a member of the banana family. Elsewhere varied leaf texture and color is provided by ferns, Dracaenas, Dieffenbachia, Gingers, and other exotics.*

71

*The colourful bracts of a Red Ginger (Alpinia purpurata) stand out against a clump of Bamboo with variegated leaves.*

*On the left along a stream grows Cyperus alternifolius, the 'Umbrella Plant', while on the right is a variegated*

dwarf Pandanus, which makes a useful ground cover. In the background can be seen Heliconia rostrata, with pendant bracts.

*The* bed on the right is accented by a tall stand of Dracaena fragrans *'Victoriae'*, which displays its colours best in full sunlight; the mass planting to the left is composed of Heliconias and Gingers.

## A Garden on Phuket

PHUKET IS A LARGE ISLAND in the Andaman Sea off Thailand's southern coast, featuring a number of spectacular beaches along its western shore as well as a few areas where the original dense rainforest cover has been retained. Rich in tin deposits, as well as rubber and coconut plantations, it enjoyed a reputation as one of the country's most prosperous provinces long before its recent emergence as a major tourist destination brought a proliferation of hotels and other resort facilities.

The property John and Pannee Ault acquired on Patong Beach in 1982 consisted of some 12 acres of disused rubber plantation and secondary forest, running along both sides of a stream that flowed all year from a mountain behind. As gardeners, they were attracted by the reliable water supply – a rarity on Phuket – plus the varied topography and the fact that the site was protected from the monsoon winds that can severely damage more exposed ornamental plants near the sea. With a team of local labourers they selectively cleared part of the property, though leaving larger trees and some handsome sugar palms, created a series of terraces leading up to the house they built, and channelled the stream to form six ponds of varying sizes. A larger part was left more or less as it was, with indigenous plants and trees, though pathways were cut through the forest and bridges built over the meandering stream.

The result is a remarkable tropical garden in which landscaped areas merge with the wild ones and the eye is constantly surprised by unexpected vistas. The Aults collected plants not only from varied parts of Thailand but also from Malaysia, Hawaii, and Australia, among other places; the garden, for example, contains more than twenty varieties of Hibiscus, as well as numerous palms,

*A Thai spirit house stands in the shade of a Cashew Nut Tree; the red bracts are those of* Alpinia purpurata, *or Red Ginger, while the variegated leaves below are* Ophiopogon. *Little houses like this, always raised on a post, are believed to shelter the guardian spirits of a compound in Thailand.*

76

including a rare one (*Karedoxa dolphin*) with silvery leaves, which is now found only in the jungles of Phuket. The smooth, sweeping lawn that sets off the massed plantings and ponds to striking effect is in fact the native wild grass that was on the original site, kept trimmed until it formed a solid cover.

One of the ponds has been devoted to day-blooming water lilies and pink lotus, while another is given over exclusively to white lotus. Beds in and around the sunny lawn are planted with various kinds of Heliconia, both double and single Hibiscus, pink and white Mussaendas, Red Ginger (*Alpinia purpurata*), Ixora, and assorted palms, while flowering trees include Lagerstroemia, Flame of the Forest (Delonix), and Jacaranda. Shadier areas contain Spathiphyllums, Cordylines, Dieffenbachias, Costus, Dracaenas, ferns and Philodendrons. Though some ornamentals have

*View from the upper level over the terraces leading down to the front of the property; the sea can be glimpsed through the coconut palms in the background. Most of the trees were on the site originally.*

Karedoxa dolphin, *a now rare palm native to Phuket which has leaves that are silvery on the bottom side; the Aults planted many of these in the jungle part of their garden.*

been introduced into the jungle part of the garden, the pathways are dominated by native Costus, ferns (including a creeping variety with iridescent blue-green leaves), towering clumps of Pandanus, wild bananas, and Ficus trees with dramatic roots.

Shortly after the photographs for this book were taken, the Ault garden was sold. It is to be hoped that the new owners will continue their horticultural work as well as their preservation of Phuket's natural landscape.

*Near the front entrance to the house, a large Ixora provides a reliable splash of colour with its clusters of scarlet flowers, while a dwarf variety of the same plant serves as a clipped hedge; a Beaumontia grows over the veranda.*

*Ponds formed by diverting the stream that flows through the garden are planted with assorted water lilies; a few clipped shrubs offer an interesting contrast to what is otherwise an informal planting against the jungle backdrop.*

*Opposite:*
*pathway leading down from the house into the jungle part of the garden; a number of ornamentals such as pink Anthurium and Dieffenbachia have been added to the indigenous plants.*

*Flower spike of a wild Costus (below).*

*A flowering wild Dracaena in the jungle area.*

*A pink-flowering Anthurium (bottom).*

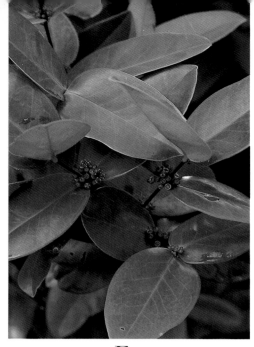

*Selaginella, a fern-like cover that grows extensively in moist areas.*

*Flowering* Mimusops elengi, *a tree native to Phuket.*

# Garden of the Prasart Museum

THE PRIVATELY OWNED PRASART MUSEUM covers some 3 acres in the Bangkok suburb of Hua Mark and was established several years ago by a former businessman named Prasart Vongsakul to display his large collection of Thai artifacts. Among the structures built on the property for this purpose are a small Buddhist chapel, a classic Thai house modelled after one in the compound of Bangkok's National Museum, an all-teakwood library set above a pond, and a European-style building evoking those that became popular in Thailand in the late 19th century. Around these examples of Thailand's religious and domestic architecture has been created a remarkable garden, combining both traditional and contemporary concepts of landscape design.

Tradition is reflected in a number of old, gnarled trees, selected as much for their form as for their flowers, and in plants that have been clipped and trained into assorted shapes. Both of these have long been features of classic Thai gardens, especially in temples and palaces, and probably evolved from Chinese influences. According to one source, the popularity of clipped trees goes back to the first Thai capital of Sukhothai; later, during the Ayutthaya period, there was a vogue for Japanese bonsais, though as M.R. Pimsai Amranand pointed out in an article on the evolution of gardens in the country, 'whereas the Japanese tried to imitate nature the Siamese tried to make their trees into odd, fantastic shapes.'

*A jungle-like atmosphere is imparted to a pathway by masses of Birds' Nest Ferns* (Asplenium nidus)*, a stand of lacy Bamboo, and, on the left,* Brassaia actinophylla, *popularly called the Octopus Tree.*

*T*hree decorative *Pigmy Date Palms* (Phoenix roebelenii) *form an effective setting for a Chinese stone figure and an antique water jar from Thailand. On the right can be seen one of the trained and clipped shrubs that are a common feature in Thai temple and palace gardens.*

86

*A* brick pathway *winds through a shady part of the garden. On the left in the background is a tall variegated* Pandanus sanderi, *below which is a Ruffled Fan Palm (*Licuala grandis*). Along the path can also be seen an Alpinia with pink bracts and a bed of* Spathiphyllum.

The gnarled trees in the Prasart garden are mostly Plumeria, or Frangipani, some of them over fifty years old, which were moved from their original locations and sited so that their odd configurations can be viewed to maximum advantage. Among the plants used for artificial shaping are *Diospyros peregrina*, a native plant with small, rough, dark-green leaves: *Wrightia religiosa*, which has delicately scented white flowers; and several varieties of Ficus with picturesque aerial roots.

Elsewhere the Prasart garden displays more contemporary tropical features, with pathways leading through miniature jungles of green- and yellow-stemmed bamboo, Heliconias, Philodendrons, Red Ginger (Alpinia), ferns, wild orchids, and brightly coloured Codiaeums, as well as a natural-looking waterfall that empties into a pool of rare red and white carp. A central lawn is devoted largely to a collection of palms.

Adding considerably to the atmosphere of the garden are items from Mr Prasart's collection. These include a number of handsome old water jars, some particularly large ones that date from the Sukhothai period and others with Chinese designs that are planted with water lilies, woodcarvings from northern Thailand, and an assortment of interesting Chinese stone figures, both human and animal. The latter became a popular feature of Thai temple and palace gardens in the early 19th century, when quantities of them came to the country on ships returning from the rice trade.

*M*alaysian *grass, a broad-leafed variety that grows in semi-shade as well as sun, borders pathways in the garden; the water jar was made in Thailand.*

89

*Sunnier parts of* the garden contain numerous shrubs clipped into formal shapes; these were characteristic of traditional Thai gardens and were probably inspired by Chinese models. There is also a wide assortment of decorative fan palms and ground covers chosen for their leaf patterns.

*A Thai temple* library overlooks a lily pond. Such libraries were traditionally built over water to protect manuscripts from white ants. On the right is a clump of wild swamp fern (*Acrostichum*) and variegated dwarf *Pandanus*.

*Some of the numerous Plumerias in the Prasart Garden, selected for their picturesque trunks as well as their flowers. The white-blooming variety has a particularly potent scent, which like most tropical flowers is strongest at night.*

*The fragrant white blossoms of Plumeria rubra.*

*Plumeria trees frame the Tamnak Daeng, an all-teak replica of a classic Thai house dating from the early 19th century; the original structure is in the compound of Bangkok's National Museum.*

Though of relatively recent origin, the Prasart Museum garden is already being acclaimed as one of the most outstanding in Thailand because of its imaginative design and varied collection of carefully selected plants. It is currently being expanded to encompass an area that will double its present size.

*A*ssorted
Bromeliads and Cordylines, both
of which thrive in Honolulu's
climate, provide year-round
colour in May Moir's courtyard
and also supply material for her
floral arrangements. Other plants
include epiphytic Staghorn Ferns
and a Tree Fern.

*F*lowers of
Medinilla magnifica,
which was introduced to Hawaii
from the Philippines.

## The May Moir Garden

BORN IN HAWAII, MRS MAY MOIR has long been prominent in local horticultural circles, both for her knowledge of plants and also for her imaginative 'flower sculptures', employing not only blooms but all sorts of plant material, which she supplies on a weekly basis to the Honolulu Academy of Arts. She has written a popular book on floral arrangement, as well as one entitled *The Garden Watcher*, a month-by-month diary describing the seasonal changes at Lipolani, her Honolulu garden in the Nuuanu Valley.

When Mrs Moir moved into her house, some forty years ago, most of the relatively small outside area was taken up by her husband's internationally celebrated orchid collection. Together the two began creating a more varied garden, an endeavour that she continued after Mr Moir's death; today relatively few of the orchids remain, mainly pink and white Phalaenopsis in a small conservatory attached to the house.

The entrance courtyard offers year-round splashes of vivid colour, thanks to massed plantings of Bromeliads together with Cordylines; in May, when the photographs for this book were

*A* small area on one side of the Moir house, visible through a large picture window, has been planted with Bromeliads in a range of subtle colours. Such plants are popular with gardeners in Hawaii for their foliage as well as for their occasional, spectacular displays of flowers.

taken, a spectacular display of showy pink blooms was also provided by a large *Medinilla magnifica*, a native of the Philippines that flowers for about two months in Hawaii. From the drawing room, a picture window divided into sections that give it the appearance of a Japanese screen looks out on more Bromeliads, the colours of which are reflected in cushions chosen for the couch. Behind the house, a shady brick terrace serves as an ideal growing environment for varied ferns, mosses, and epiphytic plants, while a more exposed area below contains an assortment of Gingers and Heliconias, many of which Mrs Moir employs in her flower arrangements.

*T*he filtered sunlight on a brick terrace behind the house provides ideal growing conditions for a variety of ferns, mosses, and epiphytic orchids.

*P*ink and white Phalaenopsis orchids cascade over potted Begonias in a conservatory attached to the house.

# Shangri-La Hotel

*A distinctive
artificial waterfall spills into a
pool in one part of the interior
hotel garden. Palms, ferns,
climbing Philodendrons,
Spathiphyllum, and other
carefully sited ornamentals
increase the jungle-like
atmosphere of the setting.*

EVEN IN A CITY NOTED FOR its imaginative public plantings, Singapore's Shangri-La Hotel has gained exceptional renown for its garden, which in turn has exerted an influence on a number of others throughout the region today.

Designed by the American firm of Bell, Collins and Associates, the Shangri-La garden is an integral part of the hotel structure, extending even up its sides through dramatic masses of Bougainvillea hanging from balconies off the rooms – perhaps the hotel's most distinctive feature – and into open-access corridors and the lobby and restaurant areas as well. One courtyard on an upper level of the ground floor has been turned into a water garden, densely planted with ground covers, palms, ferns, and other tropical exotics, and a cascade that falls into another luxuriant garden near the coffee shop below.

*Birds' Nest Ferns
(Asplenium nidus), Crinum lilies,
wild ferns, and other moisture-
loving plants enhance the effect of
an artificial stream.*

The exterior garden is divided into various sections, some, like those near the swimming pool, left relatively open with lawns and scattered coconut palms and flowering trees, and others offering a more jungle-like atmosphere with huge bamboos that were already growing on the site, Red Gingers, Heliconias, Philodendrons, and beds of white-flowering Spathiphyllum.

Reminiscent of hotel plantings in Hawaii and elsewhere in tropical America, where the same designers have worked extensively, the Shangri-La garden was one of the first to employ the concepts in Southeast Asia. Its success has led to an enhanced awareness of how greatly such integrated garden features can add beauty to an otherwise utilitarian architecture, increasingly apparent not only in many of the newer hotels but also in airports, offices, and other public buildings.

*An open outside corridor overlooks a dense planting of low ornamentals interspersed with Plumerias and toddy palms.*

*Spathiphyllum, Tree Ferns, Birds' Nest Ferns, Cordylines, and varied palms are planted in a sloping atrium garden leading down to the coffee shop.*

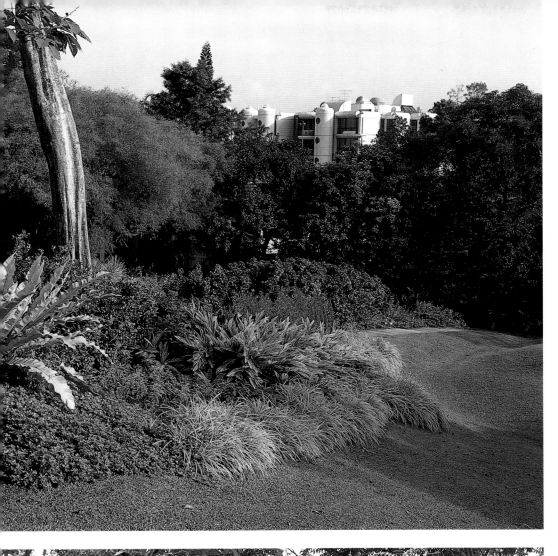

*Opposite: one of the Shangri-La's most distinctive features is its use of massed Bougainvillea in planter boxes, not only providing a dramatic display of colour but also softening the architecture and creating the effect of an almost continuous garden, vertical as well as horizontal.*

*In the outside gardens, beds of plants chosen for their contrasting leaf colours as well as flowers form islands in the lawns.*

*A view of the hotel's planter boxes; most of the exterior palms and trees were on the site when the hotel was built.*

103

## Batujimbar Gardens, Sanur Beach, Bali

MUCH OF BALI'S LEGENDARY ALLURE for Western romantics can be said to have originated at Sanur, not far from the capital of Denpasar, for it was here that some of the earliest foreign enthusiasts built bungalows on the scenic beach and produced their influential books, films, and photographs. These included Katharane Edson Mershon, a dancer-ethnologist who together with painter Walter Spies choreographed a number of still-popular Balinese dances, anthropologist Jane Belo (author of *Trance in Bali*), Vicki Baum (author of *A Tale of Bali*), and the Australian artists Donald Friend and Ian Fairweather. They were visited during the 1930s by such celebrities as Noël Coward, Charlie Chaplin, and Barbara Hutton, who also spread word of the island's unique charms.

It was Donald Friend who built the first house in what is now known as Batujimbar Estates and where, according to one account, he 'lived in imperial splendour with an in-house gamelan orchestra and Bali's finest art collection.' Today Batujimbar consists of a dozen or so private homes, each of which contains a tropical garden of exceptional beauty, sometimes separated by the coral walls characteristic of Balinese compounds and sometimes merging into common areas of lawn and massed beds of ornamental shrubs.

Tough native Pandanus with sharp serrated leaves has been planted along the sea wall as a protection against salty monsoon winds in a large central area overlooked by several houses, and Bougainvillea spills out of large stone containers on terraces. Shrubs with coloured foliage such as Cordylines, Codiaeums, Sanchezia, and Pseuderantheum, together with lower-growing covers like Scindapsus, Syngonium and Rhoeo, have been used in considerable quantities to provide contrasts in the beds, while shadier areas are planted with Red Ginger (Alpinia), Alocasia, Philodendron, and Maiden's Hair Fern for a jungle effect. Many of the plants at Batujimbar were first introduced to the island at the Bali Hyatt Hotel, which also overlooks Sanur Beach, by horticulturists who worked on both gardens.

*Lofty coconut palms provide a backdrop for a swimming pool in the garden, fed by an artificial waterfall around which grow Philodendron and gold-leafed Scindapsus. The low plant with purple leaves in the foreground is Rhoeo.*

*A* meticulously kept lawn links several gardens at Batujimbar Estate. Most of the trees were already growing on the site when the houses were built.

*B*eds of plants with coloured foliage – shrubs like Cordylines, Codiaeums, and Sanchezia and lower-growing covers like Rhoeo and Alternantheras – create islands of colour throughout the tree-dotted lawn.

*C*oconut palms, Bananas, Gingers, and other tropical specimens lend a jungle-like atmosphere to shadier portions of the estate; a native orchid grows on the trunk in the foreground.

*Balinese stone carvings, created by local artisans, line a drive in the Batujimbar Estate; spilling over a wall on the right is* Antigonon leptopus, *popularly known as the Chain of Love or Mexican Creeper, while the spiky plants in the foreground are Agaves.*

*A guest house in the garden has been transformed into a leafy pavilion with pots of giant Maidenhair Ferns, Philodendron, and other exotics that provide screening as well as a sense of tropical luxuriance. The furniture in the background is made of giant local bamboo.*

As everywhere on Bali, ponds are important features of the Batujimbar landscape design, in some cases devoted solely to pink and white lotus and in others to water hyacinth, water lettuce and papyrus. One of the swimming pools has been almost completely surrounded with tropical specimens, with a waterfall to increase its natural appearance. The houses, most of them in Balinese style with bamboo and rattan furniture, are open to allow unobstructed garden views from almost every point, and Balinese stone-carvings and lanterns are used for decoration.

Also on Sanur, just up the beach, is Tandjung Sari, a bungalow complex owned by Wiya Wawo-Runto, one of the founders of Batujimbar Estates. Established in 1962, it was one of the first resorts in the area and is still perhaps the most attractive with its series of luxuriantly planted courtyards, fern-bedecked coral walls, and extensive collection of local stone- and wood-carvings.

*A* Balinese stone figure in the garden of the Tandjung Sari, a bungalow complex on the beach near the Batujimbar Estate; the cloth around the figure has been presented as an offering.

*A*n open-roofed alcove planted with ferns and assorted creepers to create a private garden off the bathroom of a Tandjung Sari bungalow; a Balinese wood carving hangs on the brick wall.

*A* fountain in the Tandjung Sari garden, adorned with characteristic Balinese carvings and planted with Pistia, commonly called Water Lettuce.

*O*pposite: a small fishpond, fed by an artificial waterfall, is draped in a lush profusion of ferns and other tropical plants.

# The Contemporary Museum Garden, Honolulu

STILL KNOWN TO OLDER RESIDENTS as 'the Spaulding estate', after the prominent family that once owned the property and made a showplace of its garden, the Contemporary Museum is located above Honolulu on Makiki Heights Drive, a site that affords panoramic views of the city. The original design of the multi-level garden has been largely retained, though new plants have been added and some of the older ones have been clipped into geometric shapes that serve as an interesting backdrop to various pieces of modern sculpture from the museum's collection displayed throughout the grounds.

The centrepiece of the garden is a sloping lawn of remarkable smoothness, dominated by an immense umbrella-shaped Rain Tree (*Samanea saman*; known in Hawaii as Monkey-pod). Shaped plants in this and other areas include Natal Plum (*Carissa grandiflora*) and Surinam Cherry (*Eugenia uniflora*), both of which have dense leaves that make them well-suited for topiary. Below the lawn is a shadier, ravine-like lower garden, laid out along classic Japanese lines but also tropical in both plant material and atmosphere. Interesting ground covers are effectively used here along a rocky stream bed, among them *Selaginella umbrosa* (popularly called the Spikemoss plant), Peperomia with boldly patterned leaves, Rhoeo, and *Pilea nummularifolia* ('Creeping Charley'), while the steep hillsides are thickly planted with Anthuriums, Philodendrons, Heliconias, Ficus trees, and other exotics.

*A* venerable *Rain Tree (*Samanea saman*) forms its characteristic canopy over the spacious lawn of the Contemporary Museum; in the background can be seen Diamond Head and the skyscrapers of downtown Honolulu.*

*Various* evergreen shrubs have been clipped into geometrical shapes in the Contemporary Museum garden, enhancing pieces of sculpture from the collection and also creating a series of outdoor galleries.

*A* lower garden in a ravine blends Japanese landscape design with a tropical atmosphere, employing such exotics as Anthuriums and Heliconias and a wide selection of ground covers along a rocky stream bed; a Bromeliad blooms in the tree on the right.

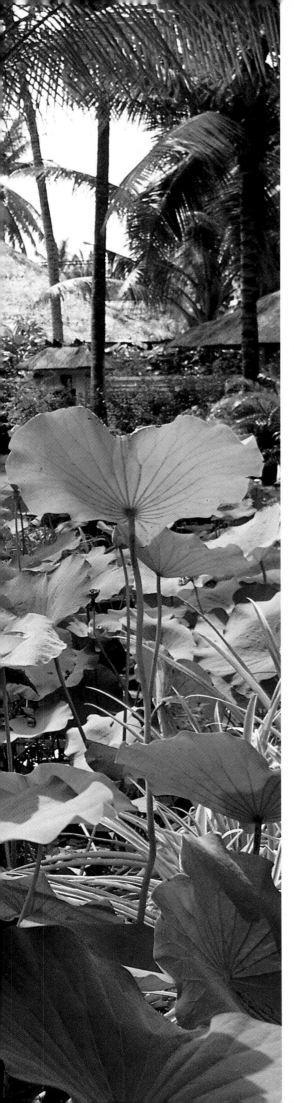

## A Bali Compound

EVER SINCE THE 1920s, when a regular steamship service was started between Bali and Java, foreigners have been attracted by the island's unique charms, and many, especially artists and scholars, have settled down for sometimes lengthy stays in Balinese homes of their own. The compound shown here, in the Sanur area, has been developed by a group of such Baliphiles, some of whom use it for holidays while others reside there more or less permanently.

Called Taman Mertasari, or 'Garden of Holy Water Essence', it contains several houses inspired by Balinese architecture as well as a traditional, thatched-roof rice barn and an open pavilion near the swimming pool. The garden, shared by all the residents, has been deliberately kept simple and open, consisting mostly of smooth lawn and tall coconut palms already on the site, with a few ornamental shrubs and hedges to provide privacy for the houses, an arrangement that requires relatively little maintenance and also allows maximum air circulation. Some palms were retained even in the large lotus pond that serves as a central feature of the compound, with earth filled in around the trunks and planted with Red Pineapple (*Ananas bracteatus*), a native of Brazil. Pathways and a terrace by the swimming pool were constructed by local artisans using slabs of volcanic stone interspersed with fine-leafed Japanese grass.

*The focal point of the garden is this large pond planted with lotus, which blooms throughout most of the year in Bali; around the palm tree in the middle is planted Red Pineapple (Ananas bracteatus).*

*The lotus, one of the most enduring symbols in Asian art from India to China.*

*A*ll of the open, Balinese-type houses in the compound have a view of the central lotus pond. The coconut palms, already growing on the

site, were incorporated into the garden design.

*S*labs of volcanic stone (top right), hewn from a

local quarry, are interspersed with a fine-leafed Japanese grass to form various walkways and terraces, illuminated at night by Balinese-style garden lamps.

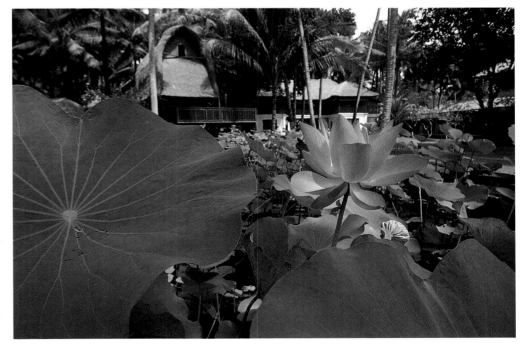

*Because of its rapidly-spreading root system, the lotus is best given a pond to itself; the flowers open in the early morning.*

# The Bali Hyatt Garden

EXTENDING OVER AN AREA of some 36 acres along Sanur Beach, the garden of the Bali Hyatt Hotel is the product of a number of designers going back to the hotel's completion in 1973. The architect, Kerry Hill of Australia, had planned for lush plantings and water gardens to soften the rather stark simplicity of the cement structure, and these were originally supplied by Ketut Relly, a Balinese graduate in landscape architecture from Trisakti University in Jakarta. An extensive revision was started in 1981 under the direction of Michael White, an Australian who is also known in Bali as Made Wijaya, and his associate Ketut Marsa. This consisted of altering some of the original planting and adding a Tropical Horticultural Garden composed mostly of decorative plants and occupying almost half of the front part of the grounds, as well as acquiring a collection of statuary and other objects by Balinese artists to place around the hotel courtyards and grounds.

The Bali Hyatt garden today is distinguished by a variety of imaginative plantings. Broad terraces in the front are planted with sweeping red, green, yellow, and variegated ground covers to create an effect of almost abstract designs, while courtyards in each wing of the hotel are based on theme plants like Hibiscus (in some places trained up a support to achieve heights of more than 20 feet), Bougainvillea, and Frangipani (Plumeria). Another series of terraces, leading down from the lobby to the swimming pool area, is given a dense tropical appearance by masses of Red Ginger (Alpinia) with exceptionally large flowers, Hibiscus, Acalypha, and Polyscias, with a number of lotus ponds and waterways. A windbreak of indigenous trees, Pandanus, and Plumeria is used along the sea front.

*Coconut palms, their trunks almost hidden by the patterned leaves of Scindapsus, tower above a profusion of Alpinia and other tropical exotics in the densely planted area below the hotel's main terrace. Many of these plants were first introduced to Bali through the hotel garden.*

*A series of broad terraces at the front of the hotel, overlooking a golf course, are* planted with multi-coloured ground covers to create a sweeping, carpet-like effect.

122

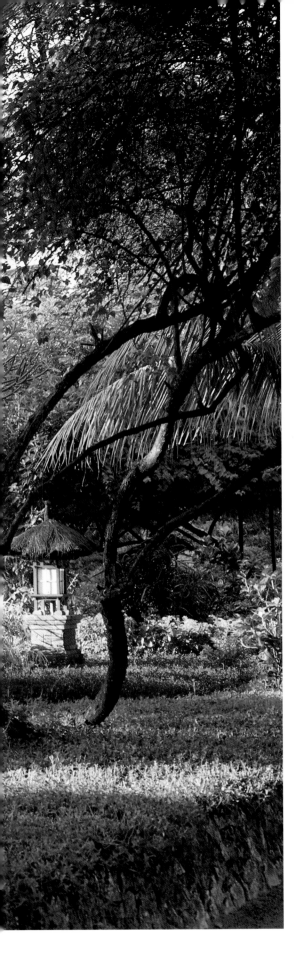

*A garden lamp, sheltered by a Balinese-style thatched roof (top), illuminates the pathways at night.*

*The rather stark lines of the hotel are softened on all sides by the lush garden (bottom); in this area clumps of* Arundodonax versicolor, *a bamboo-like reed with variegated leaves, provide a contrast to the red-leafed ground cover; an* Alpinia *blooms behind.*

*Several ponds, planted with both day- and night-blooming water lilies, add to the appeal of the Bali Hyatt's extensive garden.* Cyperus alternifolius, *Colocasia (Taro), Swamp Fern, and other water-loving plants grow in and around the ponds.*

The Horticultural Garden, where most of the specimens are labelled, contains collections of Gingers, Heliconias, Cactus, Dracaena, Crotons, Bromeliads, water plants, and palms, as well as a special garden of plants with white flowers and/or variegated leaves designed as a sort of tropical tribute to Vita Sackville-West's famous White Garden at Sissinghurst. Lawns are studded with such flowering trees as Flamboyant (*Delonix regia*), Erythrina, and Plumeria, as well as coconut palms and shady breadfruit trees.

Aside from its aesthetic appeal to guests of the hotel, the Bali Hyatt garden has also played a significant role in the introduction of many ornamental plants to Bali. A number of Gingers, Heliconias, Plumerias and other exotics, mostly brought from Singapore and Hawaii, were first cultivated at the hotel before finding their way into gardens throughout the island, adapting so luxuriantly to the fertile soil and climate that many newcomers now mistake them for indigenous plants. A small building that serves as a Horticultural Society headquarters and library on the grounds reflects this serious and continuing botanical function.

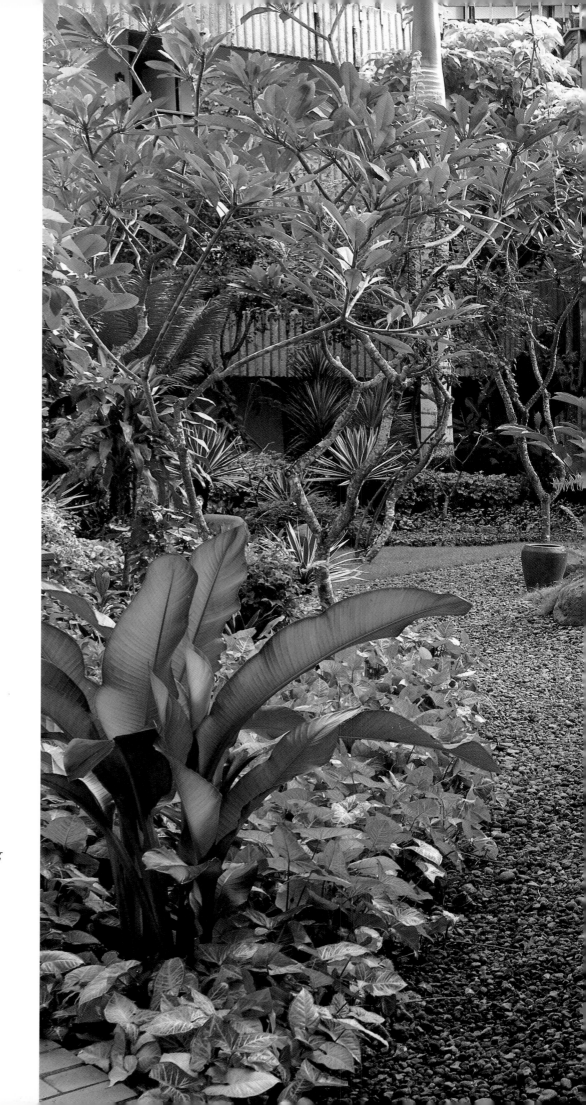

*One of the*
*interior hotel courtyards, bringing*
*the garden almost to the doors of*
*the guest rooms. A Staghorn Fern*
*hangs from the tree on the right,*
*while below it is a* Philodendron
selloum; *Syngonium is used as a*
*ground cover in the bed on the*
*left below a Heliconia with*
*bronze-coloured leaves.*

126

The 'White Garden' was planted as a tribute to Vita Sackville-West, the noted horticulturist of Sissinghurst fame. Most of the trees, shrubs, water plants, ground covers, and creepers in it have either white flowers or variegated leaves;

growing over the trellis on the left, for instance, is a white-blooming Thunbergia grandiflora Alba, while white water lilies bloom in the pond.

*O*pposite: tough indigenous trees already growing

on the site have been left along the seafront (top), where they provide shade for a pathway and protection against sea winds.

*S*hrubs with patterned leaves ensure continuous colour along the

128

garden's many walks (middle).

*Carpets of colour are achieved on stepped terraces through the use of various ground covers (bottom), mostly species of Alternanthera, which requires full sun to bring out its brightest hues.*

## *The Westin Kauai Lagoons*

THE WESTIN KAUAI LAGOONS, on the island of Kauai, is one of a new collection of hotels in the USA that offer the sort of escapist fantasy usually associated with theme parks. The lobby overlooks a two-acre reflecting pool with marble fountains and live swans; launches carry guests through a series of landscaped lagoons and waterways (where six islands are stocked with exotic wildlife); three waterfalls cascade into the vast swimming pool; and $2.5 million dollars worth of Oriental and Pacific art is lavishly scattered around the public areas.

Not surprisingly in view of its location, the hotel also contains a number of well-designed garden areas that add considerably to its romantic atmosphere. Plantings in these include massed beds of Spathiphyllum and multi-coloured Impatiens, tree ferns, Cordyline, white-flowering Datura, the so-called Blue Ginger (*Dichorisandra thyrsiflora*), Bougainvillea, and assorted Hibiscus hybrids with exceptionally large flowers. Some of the smaller gardens appear to be much larger than they are through a clever use of mirrors set into the walls.

*Swans glide across the water of the hotel's central pool; the marble horses that form part of the fountain were made to order in China.*

*Ceramic jars, set on lucite bases so that they appear to be floating, are displayed along an upper colonnade overlooking the hotel's huge swimming pool.*

*H*ibiscus and Plumbago are among the sun-loving ornamentals planted in the swimming-pool area.

*T*wo giant hybrid Hibiscus, of which the hotel has a large collection scattered through its gardens.

*Impatiens, not always an easy plant to grow in the tropics, thrives in Hawaii's mild climate. Here it is used to create a multi-coloured mass in one of the Westin Kuaui's gardens.*

Exposed hillsides outside the buildings and lagoon banks are carpeted with *Wedelia trilobata*, a tough ground cover popularly known as West Indian Creeper, which can withstand both sea winds and very dry conditions. On one hill is a stand of Norfolk Pines (*Araucaria heterophylla*), an evergreen tree that looks distinctly untropical though it is in fact native to the South Pacific and can be found in many hot-weather gardens.

133

*L*eft top: a Tree
Fern rises from a bed of
Spathiphyllum; the pendant white
flowers on the right are those of a
Datura, which in Kuaui
sometimes attains the height of a
small tree.

*L*eft *bottom: a marble figure of the Chinese goddess Kuan Yin is displayed beneath a Ficus tree at the hotel entrance; Spathiphyllum and Calathea are among the exotics used as a cover below, while the* blue flowers in the back are Dichorisandra thyrsiflora, *popularly called the Blue Ginger though in fact it belongs to the spiderwort family.*

*H*illsides around *the hotel have been planted with a variety of hardy ground covers, among them* Wedelia trilobata, *the West Indian Creeper. The trees are Norfolk Pines (*Araucaria heterophylla*), a native of the South Pacific.*

# The Leland Miyano Garden

LOCATED IN A FERTILE AREA of frequent rainfall near the foothills of the Koolaus, one of the two spinal mountain ranges on the Hawaiian island of Oahu, Leland Miyano's garden is a one-man creation that utilizes a wide variety of plants from many parts of the tropical world. The principal source, however, has been South America and especially Brazil, where Mr Miyano has gone on a number of collecting trips with his close friend and mentor Roberto Burle-Marx, the noted landscape designer responsible for many of the finest Brazilian gardens.

The Miyano garden covers only about an acre but seems much larger thanks to a creative design that utilizes winding pathways and massed plantings on hillocks and offers a series of surprising new vistas at each turn. Burle-Marx's influence is evident in the beds of swirling colour, largely provided by the showy bracts of Bromeliads and Cordylines, or Ti plants as they are known in Hawaii, in shades that range from ruby-red to flaming orange. Also outstanding are the numerous Philodendrons Mr Miyano has brought back from the South American jungles, some so recent to domestic cultivation that they have not yet been named, and a large collection of Cycads, among the oldest of the world's plants, in which he has a particular interest.

Additional noteworthy specimens used in the garden include several kinds of Heliconia, a variety of tropical iris planted around a lily pond, shrub species of both white- and purple-flowering Petrea (normally found as a creeper), a number of unusual orchids planted on rocks and tree trunks, a rare Mussaenda from Brazil with star-shaped red flowers, a Mimosa with striking cinnamon-coloured bark, and an assortment of unusual ground covers employed in effective masses along the pathways.

*Bromeliads with brightly coloured leaves have been used as a ground cover in this part of the Leland Miyano garden. The large plant in the background is a self-heading Philodendron from Brazil, while below it are some of the Cycads from Mr Miyano's large collection. A lotus grows in the water jar along with Water Lettuce (Pistia).*

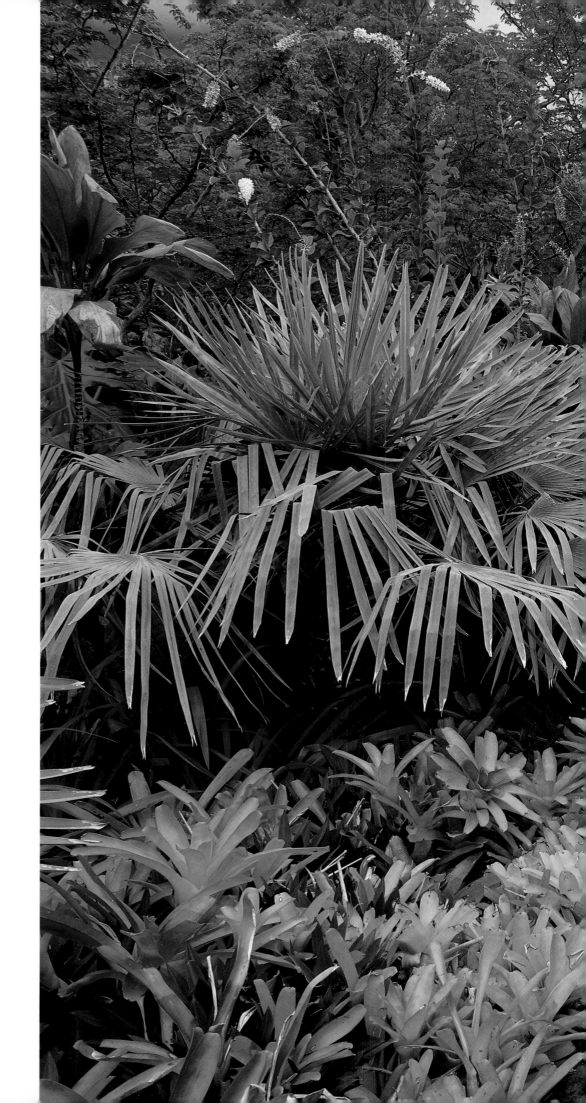

*Colour and varied leaf textures are provided by tall Cordylines, a silvery* Coccothrinax argentata *palm, assorted Bromeliads, and, on the right, two unusual Brazilian Philodendrons. Mr Miyano uses no chemical fertilizers or pesticides in his garden, relying entirely on natural methods.*

*A tropical iris* blooms on the bank of a pond, top; on the far side is a white-flowering Tabernaemontana, which resembles a small gardenia though without the strong scent, and assorted Bromeliads.

*A mixture of* Bromeliads, bottom left, with foliage of varying size and colour; the fern-like plants behind are Cycas.

*Low-growing* Cordylines, bottom right, useful as a colourful ground cover.

*Bromeliads, Cycas, Cordylines and Philodendrons growing around a small pool; a tufted, grass-like ground cover is in the foreground. The influence of Roberto Burle-Marx, the well-known Brazilian landscape architect and a friend of Mr Miyano's, is apparent in the use of brightly coloured plants and ground covers to create artistic patterns in the garden.*

In addition to the sunny main garden, there is also a sunken area that simulates humid jungle conditions through dense plantings of bananas, palms, and larger Heliconias; here Mr Miyano germinates many of the seeds he brings back from his collecting trips, especially palms, nurturing the young plants until they are ready to be tried out in other places.

A serious plant collector who has introduced a large number of new ornamentals to Hawaii, Mr Miyano is also a practising landscape designer and the garden he has achieved, largely without assistance, functions as a showcase for useful ideas in both general layout and harmonious plantings. He is a firm believer, incidentally, in the principles of organic gardening and uses neither pesticides nor chemical fertilizers in his own.

141

*Opposite: a tree in the courtyard becomes a showcase for an impressive variety of tropical exotics, among them Stag Horn Ferns, Bromeliads, and an Anthurium with large, splendidly patterned leaves.*

*An unusual Mussaenda from Brazil.*

Brassavola Digbyana; *the red leaves are Bromeliads.*

Brassavola *orchids blooming in the midst of a clump of rare Aechmea Bromeliads (below left).*

Pitcairnia *species (collected by Roberto Burle-Marx).*

Epiphytic *orchids and Bromeliads planted on rocks in one corner of the garden; in the background are Cycas and Cordylines.*

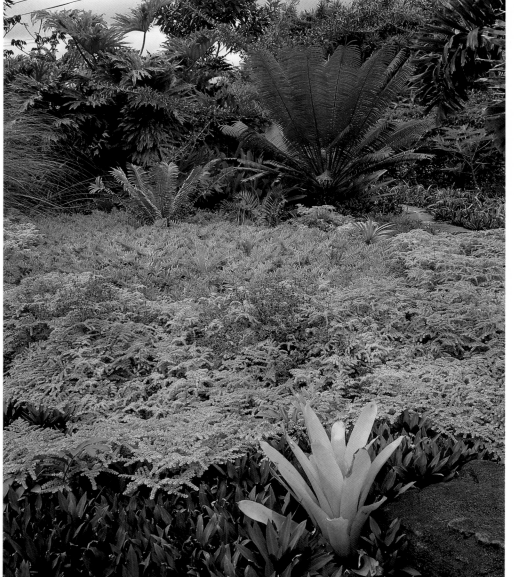

*Behind a
planting of Bromeliads, sprays of
Oncidium orchid flowers add a
bright splash of gold; in the
background are richly-coloured
Cordylines and the fern-like
leaves of a Cycad (left, top).*

*An* assortment of low-growing plants provides contrasting textures throughout the garden, sets off the distinctive shapes of larger plants, and helps the soil retain moisture in dry periods (left, below).

*Rhoeo* is used as an effective ground cover along this stone pathway, while the spiky leaves of Bromeliads and Cycads give colour and height to the landscape. The long feathery leaves in the background on the right are those of a 'Pony-tail Palm' (Beaucarnea recurvata).

145

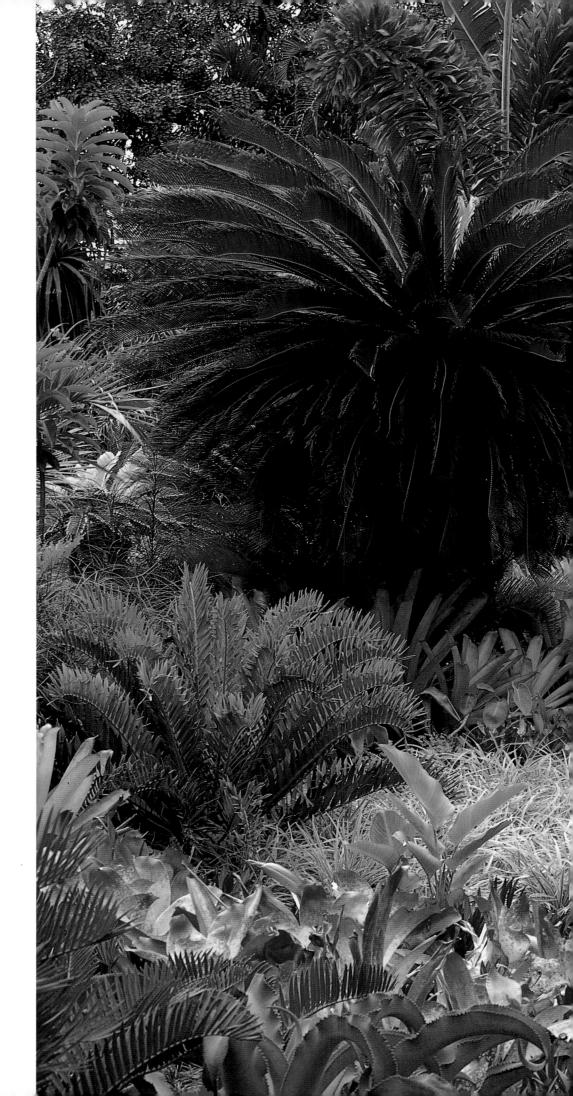

*Striking patterns are created through the careful use of varicoloured ground covers. On the left in the background is a giant Cycad, one of the earliest plants to appear on earth, while on the right is a pair of Traveler's Palms* (Ravenala), *a native of Madagascar which acquired its popular name because fresh water collects at the bases of the leaves and can be drunk by thirsty wanderers.*

# The Allerton Gardens

*The lawn in front of the Allerton house stretches down to a private beach, at the mouth of a river valley on the west coast of Kauai.*

KAUAI, HAWAII'S OLDEST POPULATED ISLAND, is a place of dramatic volcanic scenery and climatic contrast. Waialeale, at its eastern end, is known as the wettest spot on earth, with an annual rainfall of some 500 inches, while the western side is almost desert at higher elevations; a number of the native birds and plants on Kauai are found nowhere else in the islands, thanks to sanctuaries provided by high mountains and dense jungle canyons, and it is ringed with sandy beaches of exceptional beauty.

The Allerton gardens, located in a verdant valley on the west coast, were started by Queen Emma, wife of King Kamehameha IV, who lived on the picturesque seaside site until 1875. An enthusiastic gardener, Queen Emma introduced a large number of ornamental specimens to the island, including a mass planting of Bougainvillea which cascades down a cliff behind the present house. After her death, the property was acquired by Alexander McBryde, a noted horticulturist, who enlarged the plant collection and laid out the garden along its present lines.

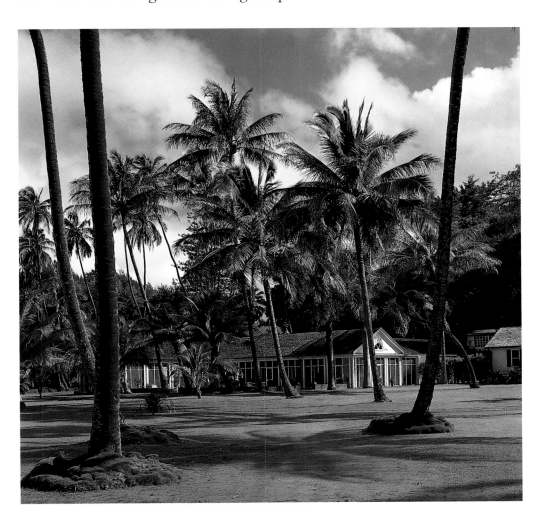

*Coconut palms shade the lawn of the Allerton house, behind which lie the gardens created by Robert Allerton and his son John Gregg Allerton over a span of some fifty years.*

*Scarlet* Clerodendron *flowers add colour to one of the densely planted pathways on a hillside; Philodendrons climb in the trees above and form a cover on the slope.*

*This elongated shallow pool, on several different levels, is one of the several striking water features in the Allerton gardens.*

In 1938 the lower end of the Lawai valley, which includes the property, was purchased by Robert Allerton, originally as a winter home. His son John designed the house and together with his father travelled widely to collect more plants; they also added a number of pools, waterfalls, and architectural features to the gardens. After inheriting the estate, John Gregg Allerton continued to improve the extensive gardens and lived there until his own death in 1989. The property, now under the supervision of Mr Toshi Kaneko, who worked with Mr Allerton for many years, was bequeathed to the adjoining Pacific Tropical Botanical Gardens, whose aims include the preservation of endangered tropical plants and research into species of medicinal and economic value.

Lawai Kai, as the gardens are called, covers a large area on both sides of a wide stream flowing through the valley to the sea, and enjoys an unusually varied topography that includes open meadows, moist jungled ravines, and hills rising to considerable heights. These, together with Kauai's rich volcanic soil, offer ideal growing conditions to a wide selection of plants and trees and made

151

The Mermaid
Fountain empties into an Art
Deco zigzag channel, making an
imaginative artistic statement
against the tropical mass of
Rhapis palms. The mermaid
figures are identified as having
been made by a Florentine
sculptor named Andreotti in 1931.

Overleaf
(pp.154–155): a serene, latticed
pavilion overlooks the Diana
Fountain on one of the garden's
upper levels. Most of the statuary
was acquired by the Allertons on
trips to Europe.

it possible for the Allertons to create a garden — more precisely, a series of gardens linked by pathways — of imaginative design and exceptional botanical interest. One section, for instance, is largely devoted to an impressive collection of Heliconias, Costus, Calathea, and Gingers while another contains mainly different species of giant bamboo. Hillsides are planted with either Cassias of assorted hues (known as Shower Trees in Hawaii, where they are frequently used to line streets) or varied Plumerias, and on the exposed cliff overlooking the sea are cacti (including a low wall of night-blooming Cereus) and Bougainvillea.

Scattered throughout in strategic clearings, the gazebos, pools, fountains, and statuary (which ranges from classical to Art Deco) add to the charm of Lawai Kai without detracting from the generally natural atmosphere that gives it such distinction.

*Y*ellow Bamboo (Phyllostachys) *creates a dimly lit forest in an area devoted to various species of Bamboo. Elsewhere in the garden are comprehensive collections of other tropical plants and flowering trees.*

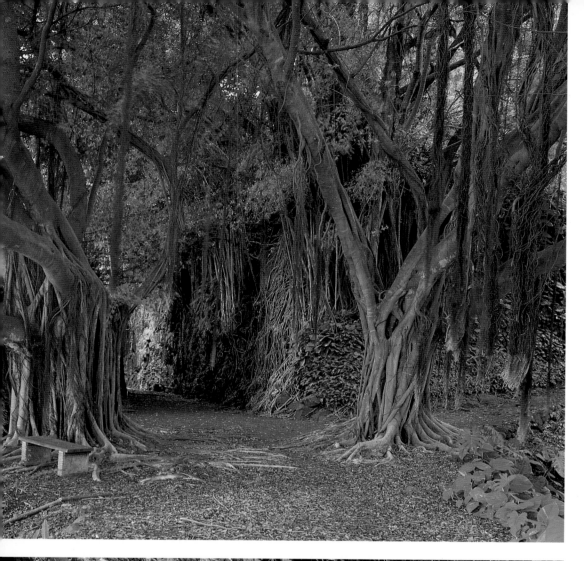

*The twisted roots of aged Ficus trees form odd patterns near the top of a towering cliff in the Allerton gardens.*

*Perpetually dripping water creates an ideal environment for a wall of ferns, moss, and tropical creepers along a road leading to the upper reaches of the gardens.*

*Giant Anthuriums border a stream that cascades over successive levels down a hillside; thanks to such features the restful sound of running water is audible in almost every part of the extensive gardens.*

## The Victor Sassoon Garden

*I*n the foreground can be seen the huge leaves and a freshly opened flower of Victoria Amazonica, *the great Brazilian water lily that became the rage of Victorian England when one flowered in a special glasshouse at Chatsworth. Beyond, a lawn of Malaysian grass leads to the rear terrace of the Sassoon house.*

VICTOR SASSOON'S GARDEN – an unusually large one for a private compound in present-day Bangkok – has been developed over some 25 years. Trees, coconut and fishtail palms, and tall stands of bamboo provide an effective screen on three sides of the property, creating a rare green oasis in a residential district now largely dominated by impersonal high-rise condominiums.

Already on the site, mostly near the house, were a number of mature trees, among them Mango, Tamarind, and Flamboyant (*Delonix regia*), and to these have been added *Tabebuia rosea, Pterocarpus indica, Lagerstroemia floribunda*, and *Peltophorum inerme* (Yellow Poinciana). Flowering shrubs and exotics planted in beds include several species of Hibiscus, dwarf Ixora (trimmed to form a hedge along the drive), varied Heliconias, *Sanchezia nobilis*, Spathiphyllum, Dieffenbachia, and assorted Philodendrons, while among the creepers on fences and trellises are Bougainvillea, *Petrea volubilis, Thunbergia grandiflora, Cleloden-dron splendens*, and *Solandra nitida*. A large L-shaped pond at the rear of the garden contains *Victoria Amazonica* as well as smaller water lilies in various colours. On a terrace, potted plants – among them large hybrid Spathiphylum, Maidenhair ferns, Hibiscus, Bougainvillea, and Heliconias with showy green-and-yellow leaves – have been massed to create a luxuriant tropical atmosphere reflecting that of the garden as a whole.

*S*pathiphyllums *provide a setting for an antique water jar used as decoration in the garden.*

*P*otted ferns and
assorted foliage plants bring the garden
onto the terrace near the front
entrance, shaded by a Mango tree.

Heliconia
illustris, *grown for its colourful
leaves rather than its flowers
(left), adds to the colour of the*

terrace pot plants; on the right is
a hybrid Spathiphyllum which
has exceptionally large blooms. In
the background is an aviary.

*Dwarf Ixora has
been clipped to form a neat hedge
along the driveway.* Solandra
guttata, *popularly called the Cup*

of Gold, grows over the trellis,
while a mass of Heliconias is on
the right. The tree shading the
area is a Ficus benchamina.

163

## Bangkok Hilton International Garden

THE HILTON INTERNATIONAL HOTEL IN BANGKOK was built partly on the site of a pleasure garden created in the early years of this century by a prominent businessman named Nai Lert; the area was then on the outskirts of the city, accessible only by canal, and the garden, popularly known as Nai Lert Park, was used as a weekend retreat. When Nai Lert's daughter, Khunying Lurasakdi Sampati-siri, decided to develop the property in the mid-1980s, she redesigned a part of the park and incorporated it into the hotel grounds, creating one of the largest semi-private gardens in central Bangkok today.

Water is a prominent feature of the garden, with two ponds – the larger planted with *Victoria Amazonica* water lilies – and an artificial waterfall of impressive dimensions. Most of the plants came from Khunying Lurasakdi's own large collection and include an unusually wide variety of trees, shrubs, climbers, and ground covers, most labelled with their Thai and botanical names. Among the flowering trees are Jacaranda, Delonix (including one with unusual apricot-coloured flowers), both white- and red-blooming Erythrina, Bauhinia (Orchid Tree), *Peltophorum inerme* (Yellow Poinciana), *Saraca indica*, Plumeria, Tabebuia, and several kinds of Cassia, one of which (*C. fistula*, or Golden Shower) is Thailand's national tree. Shady areas are planted with Philodendron, ferns, and various foliage plants, while such shrubs as Ixora (in red, pink, white, and orange), Oleander, Hibiscus, Lantana, Jasmine, and Gardenia grow in sunnier parts. Climbers include *Petrea volubilis*, with purple sprays that resemble Wisteria; Bougainvillea in assorted colours; *Beaumontia grandiflora*, which has huge clusters of fragrant white flowers; and a climbing Bauhinia with white flowers and fern-like leaves.

Spacious in size, the Hilton International garden nonetheless manages to suggest the intimate atmosphere of a personal creation, thus preserving a link with its origins nearly a century ago.

*Ordinary water lilies and, in the background, the giant* Victoria Amazonica *grow in the main pond of the Hilton garden. On the opposite bank is a large* Pandanus sanderi *with variegated leaves.*

165

*A* bridge spans one of the garden's waterways, beneath a canopy of coconut palms and flowering trees.

B ixa orellana, *popularly called the Lipstick Plant.*

A calypha hispida, *the Chenille Plant.*

*An artificial waterfall, shaded by a small jungle of Ficus trees and Bamboo, forms one of the most striking landscape features in the Hilton garden.*

## The Singapore National Orchid Garden

TOWARDS THE END OF THE 19TH CENTURY, a Singapore resident named Miss Agnes Joaquim discovered an unknown orchid blooming in her garden. She took it to the Director of the Botanical Garden, who confirmed that it was indeed unknown to science, a natural hybrid between *Vanda hookerana* and *V. teres*, and announced it in 1893. Within a few years what he called *Vanda Miss Joaquim* was being widely distributed by the Garden and had become a favourite with local gardens; it is today Singapore's national flower.

Orchids had long been a prominent feature in the Botanical Garden – by 1912, 276 species were being displayed, the largest number of any plant group – and under the directorship of Eric Holttum (1925–49), orchid hybridizing became a major activity at the gardens. The Orchid Enclosure, rebuilt in the postwar years, displayed more than 12,000 plants, ranging from wild species to such hybrids as *Dendrobium Margaret Thatcher* (introduced in 1985), and was undoubtedly the most popular attraction with visitors. To accommodate more specimens, a new enclosure known as the National Orchid Garden was opened in 1995 by Dr Tan Wee Kiat, the current Director, and his team. Only a year after its completion, the enclosure already seemed an integral part of Southeast Asia's most beautiful Botanical Garden.

*The display of hybrid and wild orchids is regularly changed to ensure a wide variety of flowering specimens in the enclosure.*

*Ground orchids are massed in an impressive display; the fan palms that provide dramatic focal points are Pritchardias (right).*

*A hillside path leading to the Orchid Enclosure. A Casuarina tree grows beside the fountain, while Cordylines line the path on the far side; the tree on the right is an Erythrina.*

*Orchids on display; at the top is a Dendrobium hybrid, while the other two are Vanda hybrids.*

170

*T*owering
*Ceiba, or kapok, trees near the
main house, grown from seeds
collected in Venezuela.*

*A* flowering
*Dalbergia, a native Thai tree.*

## A Forest Garden in Central Bangkok

TOWARDS THE END OF WORLD WAR II, when Allied bombers began to target sites in the older part of Bangkok, a Thai Muslim family sought refuge by moving to a suburb then accessible only by boat along one of the city's larger canals. The move was regarded as temporary but by the time the war ended all of them, particularly the elder son Hajji Prayoon Vadanyakul, had grown fond of the large, peaceful area they had acquired. Hajji Prayoon planted fruit trees, began to raise fish in ponds, married, and settled down. 'People couldn't understand why he wouldn't move back to the city,' says his daughter Prabhadibhaya, 'He told them, "Don't worry, the city will soon follow me here."'

173

*Crescenta alata,*
*a tree on which the flowers*
*appear on the trunk (below, top).*

*Massive*
*buttress roots of a wild tree in the*
*garden (bottom).*

*Parmentiera*
cereifera, *the 'Candle Tree' (top).*

*Fruit of* Kigelia
pinnata, *the 'Sausage Tree'*
*(middle).*

*Flowers of*
Kigelia pinnata *(bottom).*

*O*ne of the ponds in the garden, originally dug to raise fish (above).

*S*piny trunk of Salmalia, a native Thai tree of the Bombax family (below).

Hajji Prayoon lived to see his prophecy come true. The city did indeed follow, and now the area is one of Bangkok's most crowded. The canal survived, however, and so did Suan Sa-ngob, or 'Tranquil Park', as the estate is called, a leafy oasis of tall trees and birdsong that covers several acres. The original fruit trees have been joined by a comprehensive botanical collection, not only of native trees and plants but others gathered on trips abroad, carefully labelled with their Latin names.

'High-rise buildings may take just a few years to build,' reads a sign in the garden. 'But a tree takes years to grow tall . . . The aim of Suan Sa-ngob is to preserve Thailand's flora in an age when forest after forest is being destroyed. It is hoped that the trees grown here will be a source of knowledge for those who study them and a source of pleasure for those who see them.'

Hajji Prayoon's family have been offered huge sums for the valuable property. They prefer, however, to keep their Tranquil Park as an enduring symbol of what has been lost in so much of modern Bangkok.

## Two Singapore Gardens

MICHAEL WHITE, also known by his Indonesian name of Made Wijaya, has designed a number of Singapore's most outstanding gardens, both public and private. In addition to the landscape, usually lush and tropical, he also plays a prominent role in planning such features as terraces, courtyards, pools, and garden decorations, the latter often supplied by a recently launched venture called Wijaya Classics.

*Swimming pool in a hilltop garden; palms and a stand of Traveller's Palms (*Ravenala madagascariensis*) enhance the tropical feeling (left and below). Garden ornaments were made in Bali for Wiyaya Classics, a collection which was launched in this garden.*

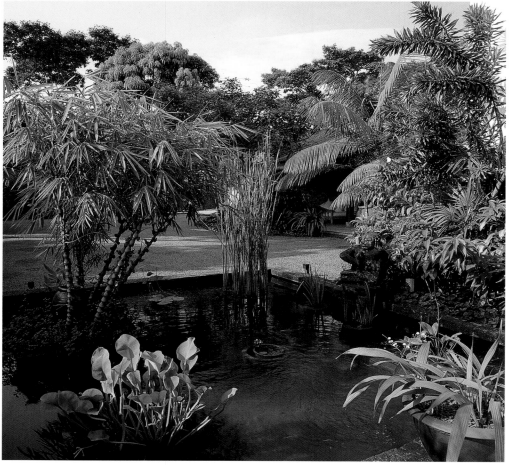

*P*ots *from West Java serve as ornaments in this area; growing in the tree is a Bird's Nest Fern, the white flowering plant on the right is Hymenocallis (left, top).*

*A formal pool is planted with a variety of bamboo popularly known as 'Buddha's Belly' and tall* Typha angustifolia, *and* Echinodorus cordifolius *(below).*

*View of the garden from the patio; ground orchids bloom in the pot, while other plants include Hymenocallis and Cordyline and the tree is a red-flowering Erythrina (above).*

The two private gardens on these and the following pages are unusually spacious for modern Singapore, where large pieces of residential land have become rare. In one, a dramatic swimming pool – inspired by Peter Mueller's design for the Amandari Hotel pool in Bali – seems to empty from the top of a steep hillside, surrounded by luxuriant foliage, while in the other, sun-dappled views of the garden form a restful panorama outside the cool, tiled patio of a house designed by the architect Ernesto Bedmar. In both, it is difficult to believe that the skyscrapers of downtown Singapore rise just a short drive away.

## A Rooftop Garden in Singapore

SINGAPORE'S URBAN REDEVELOPMENT AUTHORITY occupies an eight-storey building in the city's central business district. Since there was no available space for a ground-level garden, it was decided to have one on the roof, convenient to such facilities as a canteen and squash courts, and thus provide an additional recreational area for the staff as well as an area of green to relieve the surrounding views.

Designed by Michael White and installed by his local partner, Fairuz Salleh, the garden consists of a group of raised containers, each surrounded by benches and planted with a variety of tropical ornamentals. One, for example, contains a pentagonal pool with a fountain in the centre and is sheltered by a vine-covered wooden trellis, a pleasant place to rest during lunch breaks or after work. According to White, the area was particularly designed for evening use by URA employees who work late or stay on to relax.

*A fountain* provides the soothing sound of water in a pool surrounded by benches. The water plants include Pontederia cordats, *with attractive heart-shaped leaves, and* Cyperus alternifolius, *a close relative of Egyptian Papyrus.*

*A lattice roof* shelters raised planter beds in the URA rooftop garden; on the lower right is a Spider Lily (Hymenocallis), *while the tree is a Plumeria (above).*

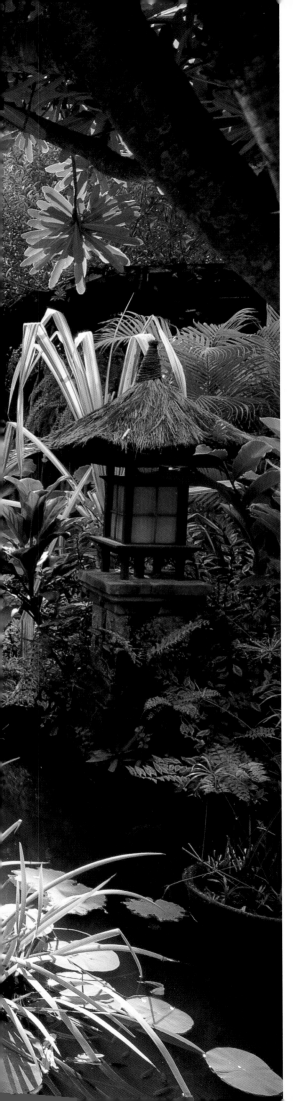

## The Made Wijaya Garden

MADE WIJAYA, OR MICHAEL WHITE as he was known in his native Australia, has been a resident of Bali since 1973. The first garden he planted was for his own house, in Sanur, which attracted so much admiration that he eventually gave up other pursuits to become a full-time landscape designer. In all he has been responsible for more than 300 projects, not only in Bali – where his work includes the landmark Bali Hyatt gardens and those for the newer Four Seasons Resort – but also elsewhere in Indonesia, Singapore, Thailand, and as far afield as the Caribbean home of the pop star David Bowie.

His current residence, the Villa Bebek, which also serves as an office, workshop, and testing place for garden ideas, is a typically Balinese arrangement of courtyards, water features, and planting that achieves a jungle-like effect while in fact being carefully controlled. (Wijaya refers to it jokingly as 'the tropical Cotswolds look'.) Lily ponds reflect the tall coconut palms of a surrounding plantation, Bougainvillea

*B*alinese girls *in traditional dress make an offering beside a water-lily pond in one of the courtyards at the Villa Bebek.*

*A pathway of stone set into grass leads to one of the thatched-roof Balinese buildings (below); the tall plant with white and green striped leaves on the left is* Pandanus veitchii, *while the flowers on the right are a Bougainvillea.*

*Swimming pool of the Villa Bebek; a white-flowering* Thunbergia grandiflora *is planted over the pergola, and a Plumeria grows on the right.*

brings a splash of colour to high stone walls, Plumerias and various shrubs scent the air, and lanterns with thatched roofs cast a soft glow when evening falls. A swimming pool area is more open, mainly planted with palms and smaller trees, and has a pergola covered with white-flowering *Thunbergia grandiflora.* Scattered throughout are numerous intriguing art objects, some primitive works collected in various parts of Indonesia and other contemporary creations produced by ten local sculptors who work for Wijaya in the compound.

*Decorative Water Lettuce (*Pistia stratiotes*) grows in a jar around a stone sculpture; on the left is an Adenium (below, top).*

*View of the pool from the pergola; planting in this courtyard has mostly been kept low to allow more sunlight (bottom).*

*View of a courtyard pond from Made Wijaya's office. The statue is a copy of one by the late Brett Whiteley, a noted Australian sculptor. The pond is planted with water lilies and lotus; the pink-flowering plant on the right is Adenium coetaneum.*

*A collection of primitive sculptures from eastern Indonesia; on the right is a variegated Crinum (right, top).*

*The sculptures are displayed on a raised bed of grass supported by local stones (middle).*

*A thatched-roof lantern illluminates a lily pond*

(bottom). The round stone in the foreground is known as an 'earth button' and is placed at the centre of a circle of wedge-shaped rice fields in Indonesia.

## The Four Seasons Resort Bali

ONE OF THE MORE SPECTACULAR BALINESE GARDENS planted in recent years is that of the Four Seasons Resort at Jimbaran, on the semi-arid Bukit Peninsula. Covering some 35 acres along a scenic coastal site, with distant views of volcanoes across the sea, the resort has been conceived as a series of seven Balinese villages, connected by garden walks. Australian architects Martin Grounds and Jack Kent were responsible for the architectural work, while the tropical gardens were designed by Made Wijaya (Michael White). The project took nearly two-and-a-half years to complete and the landscape is today maintained by over 100 gardeners.

Wijaya has used a core of local plants in the gardens, supplemented by other ornamental species adapted to the dry location. An alert visitor may also notice that 'seasons' vary over the extensive site: a tree in early flower in one area may be in full fruit elsewhere, offering an instructional lesson in Bali's botanical diversity during a stroll through the villages.

*P*rivate pool of an individual villa at the Four Seasons Resort (left). The poolside planting includes a variegated form of Pedilanthus, Bougainvillea, and Plumeria, all drought-resistant specimens. In the background can be seen Gunung Agung, Bali's most sacred volcano.

As in many seaside gardens, drought-resistant plants play a major role in the design. These include Bougainvillea, originally from the American tropics, which blooms best under dry conditions; spiky Agaves with bold green-and-white leaves; fragrant Plumeria, essentially a desert tree in its native Central America; hardy Adeniums with prominent pink flowers; and *Russelia equisetiformis*, the Coral Plant, a popular rock garden specimen with long, drooping branches and a continual display of small, bright-red flowers. Closer to the sea, such plants as Pandanus and cactus can withstand even the saltiest sea winds.

Contributing to the atmosphere of the resort are numerous architectural features and garden ornaments. The thatched-roof, open lobby pavilion, for example, has commanding views of Jimbaran Bay and the sacred volcano Gunung Agung, Bali's spiritual heart, while each individual villa is located in a separate compound with its own entrance

*P*isonia, the Lettuce Tree, Bougainvillea, and yellow Allamanda are some of the specimens that bring colour to this walkway, overlooked by a stone Buddha image.

*D*ramatic stonework gives architectural definition to the garden, softened by such plants as wild Dracaena, Plumeria, and bright Bougainvillea (opposite, top).

*V*illas at the resort have panoramic sea views, while the thatched roofs and linking walkways create a village-like atmosphere.

190

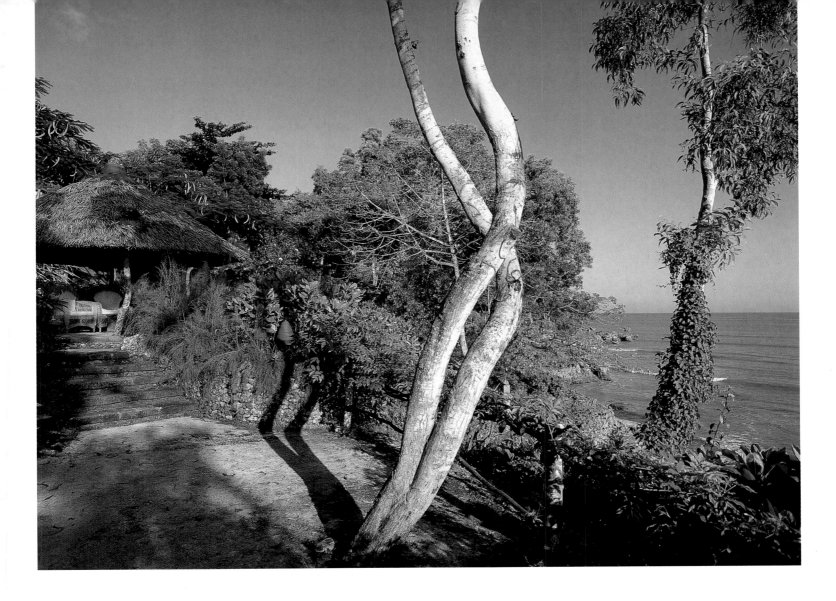

*Native trees were incorporated into the garden design, as in this hill overlooking the sea.*

*Introduced ornamentals like Russelia, which spills over the stone wall leading to a pavilion, have been combined with indigenous species to give a natural look in many areas.*

gate. A local village temple was restored during construction of the resort and is the scene of frequent ceremonies. Among the decorative objects are stone statues and bas-reliefs carved by local artisans, huge water jars, and an assortment of traditional lanterns.

R̲usselia
equisetiformis *is planted in
raised beds so that its long,
dropping branches and red*

flowers can be seen to maximum advantage (left, top and below). The white-flowering tree in the background is a Plumeria.

*T*all wild Dracaena, Russelia, green-and-white Agave, Cycads, Bougainvillea, and other hardy

plants can be seen on a hillside overlooking the sea (above).

*Swimming pool* of the resort, which seems to spill over the edge of the hill, a design that has become popular in resorts.

*Stone pathway* connecting various parts of the resort (right, top); Phoenix palms are planted on the left, while red-flowering Russelia is on the right.

*Pandanus, Plumeria, and Bougainvillea form a background for this swimming pool (middle).*

*A fragrant white Plumeria is planted on an artificial island in one of the pools (bottom).*

# Garden Features

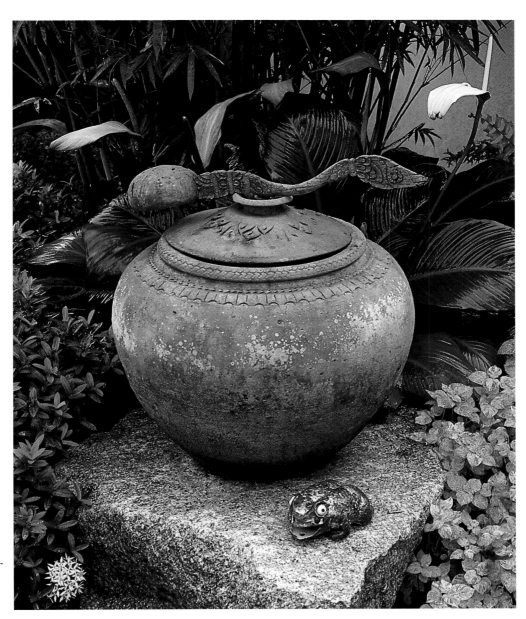

*A modern Thai earthenware jar used as a garden ornament.*

*Courtyard of the Hart and Tagami Gallery in Hawaii.*

*In tropical as in temperate gardens, the ultimate success of a landscape design depends not only on the selection and arrangement of plant materials but also on the skill with which assorted features are employed to enhance its natural beauty. A path or walkway of unusual design and texture, a fence or wall that manages to be attractive as well as practical, a strategically sited gazebo, an imaginative use of statuary and lighting fixtures, ornamental fountains, pools, or even extensive artificial lakes — all can be vital in creating the special atmosphere that makes a particular garden memorable.*

# Pathways

WALKWAYS ARE NOT ONLY ESSENTIAL to most garden designs but also add to – or in some cases detract from – their overall effectiveness. An interesting pattern of bricks or other material can turn a path into more than simply a means of getting from one part of the landscape to another, just as it can give character to a poolside terrace or courtyard; on the other hand, the unimaginative use of cement can destroy what might otherwise be a pleasing view or atmosphere. Of equal importance is the choice of plants that border such obviously man-made features, either disguising and softening the edges or giving them emphasis.

*S*ections of a tree trunk are used as stepping stones in a garden in northern Thailand.

*P*athways at the Amandari Hotel in Bali form interesting geometric patterns as they cross a courtyard. The garden was designed by Made Wijaya.

*Pebbles and larger stones form swirling designs in the courtyard of the Han Snel Guest House in Ubud, Bali; a hanging Heliconia blooms against the wall in the background.*

*A pathway in the garden of Bangkok's Oriental Hotel.*

*A rustic path, bordered by a variegated ground cover, in Java's Cibodas Botanical Garden.*

*A patterned brick walkway in a Malaysian resort.*

# Garden Ornaments

THE VARIETY OF STRUCTURES, statuary, and other decorative garden features is almost endless, with the choice depending mainly on individual taste. Larger areas can accommodate an ornamental pavilion, orchid house, or aviary, while almost any landscape can be improved through strategically sited stone, wood, metal, or ceramic figures, large water jars planted with lilies or displayed merely as objects of beauty, garden furniture of pleasing and harmonious design, and distinctive works of art that reflect local culture or that are created especially for the space in which they are used.

*Opposite: an antique Chinese statue; a ceramic fish made in northeastern Thailand; a stone figure of the Hindu god Ganesha.*

*A northern-style Thai spirit house in the Bangkok garden of Mr and Mrs Yvan Van Outrive.*

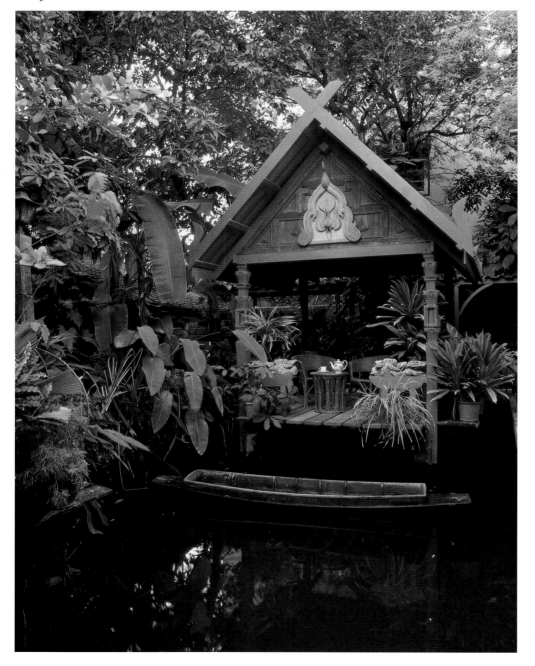

*A Thai-style pavilion built over a pond in a Bangkok garden.*

*O*rnamental
*figure in Singapore's Botanical
Garden.*

*Painted water jars at the Oriental Hotel's Chinese restaurant.*

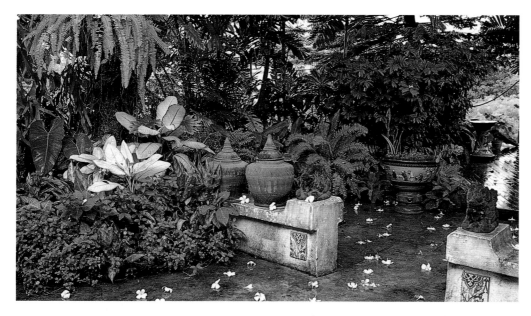

*Glazed tiles set in the wall of a Singapore garden.*

*Sunken jars used for growing water lilies.*

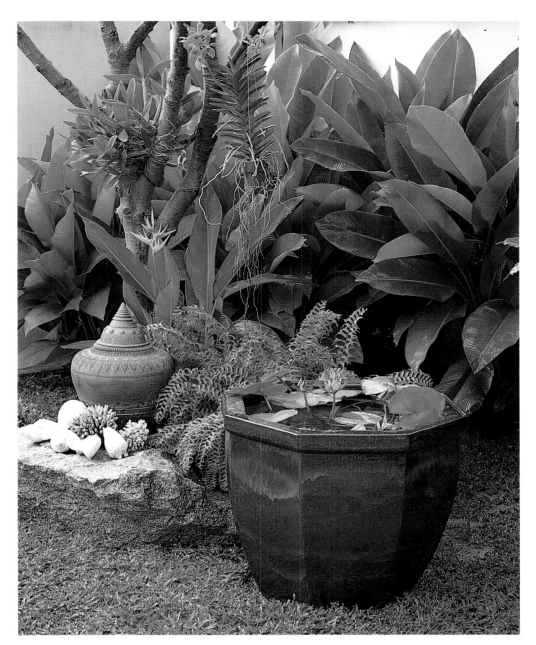

*A*gainst a luxuriant background of Heliconia, an antique water jar is used as a container for Nymphaea; placed with shells and coral on the stone on the left is an earthenware Thai jar.

*A* huge, elegantly-shaped 14th-century water jar from Sukhothai, the first Thai capital, serves as a dramatic focal point on a lawn containing various palms in a Bangkok garden.

## Walls and Fences

*A stone wall planted with assorted Bromeliads at the Kahala Hilton Hotel in Honolulu.*

IF WALLS AND FENCES do not make for good neighbours, such barriers are nonetheless necessary in most gardens, tropical or otherwise, not only to delineate property but also to screen out certain areas. They can be enhanced in a number of ways, however: by almost covering them with a luxuriant display of plants, by building on a series of levels so that the wall becomes a part of the garden, or, perhaps most common of all, by accentuating them through the use of imaginative materials – bamboo, for instance, or coral, as in the case of most Balinese walls, or with insets of ceramic tiles – to create a pleasing architectural pattern.

*F*icus pumila *creeps across a wall of* closely fitted stones.

*A* Balinese wall made with thin slabs of volcanic stone.

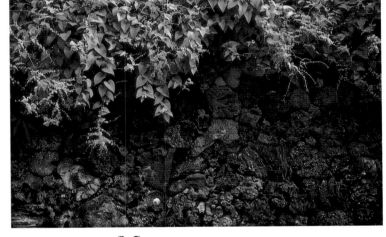

*A* patterned wall made of coral in a Balinese garden.

*A* wall in Bali, fashioned from slabs of lava stone, with assorted plants growing in the crevices.

*M*exican Creeper (Antigonon leptopus) on a wall of black coral.

*A* stone wall almost covered with the roots of a Ficus tree.

*P*ierced, glazed Chinese tiles create an interesting decorative pattern, and also allow air circulation, when incorporated into a wall like this one in Bali.

*A* fence of bamboo in contrasting patterns serves as a screen as well as a decorative feature in the garden of Bangkok's Oriental Hotel; a modern Thai jar is on the left.

*R*ustic fences of split bamboo, at once attractive and inexpensive, are commonly seen in rural Thailand; this one is in a garden in the northern town of Lampang.

*A trim white wooden fence borders a flight of steps leading down a steep hillside to a garden in Honolulu; the walls are thickly covered with Ficus pumila.*

*A massive effect is created by a wall made of cement and volcanic stone bordering a walkway at Bali's Amandari Hotel, designed by Australian architect Peter Muller.*

## Pools, Fountains, and Waterfalls

WHETHER MODEST OR SPECTACULAR, ornamental pools, fountains, and waterfalls have been a prominent part of tropical gardens since antiquity and continue to be so today. A decorative pool may be severely formal, an architectural extension of the buildings around it, or natural-looking with carefully selected rocks and plants, while fountains can be fashioned from a wide variety of objects as suggested in those shown here. Similarly, the restful sound of water cascading down over different levels can be achieved even without topography through ingenious methods that disguise their artificiality.

*An unusual fountain made of stacked ceramic pots, in a northern Thai garden; formal, clipped plants, a traditional Thai specialty, are in the background.*

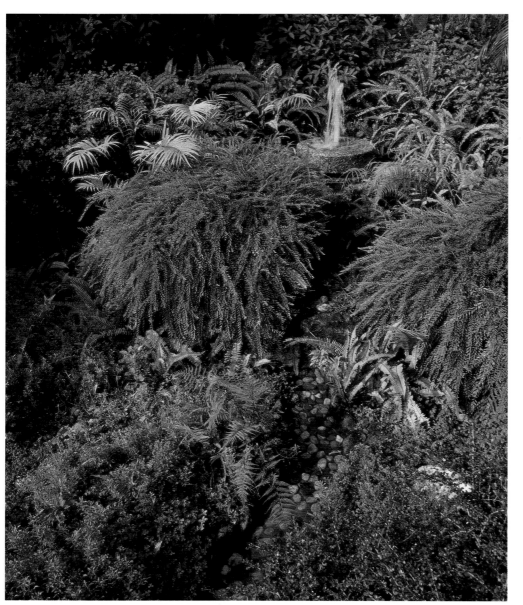

*An old grindstone, once used by Chinese who came to work in local tin mines, forms the base of a fountain in the Ault Garden at Phuket; water power is supplied by a stream flowing through the property.*

*A* series of pools, one flowing into another, in the garden of M.L. Tri Devakul at Phuket.

*A*n artificial waterfall, spilling into a pool of ornamental carp, in the garden of the Prasart Museum in Bangkok.

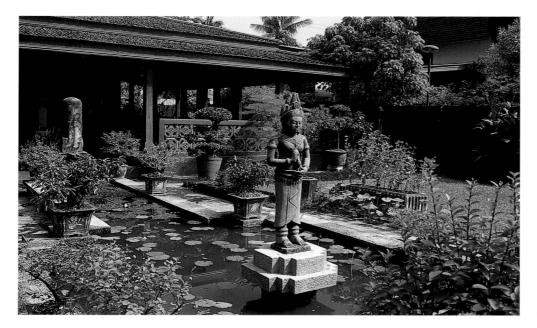

*Khmer figures in a geometric pond in the garden of M.R. Kukrit Pramoj in Bangkok.*

*A pond bordered by slabs of laterite, planted with tall, blue-flowering Thalia geniculata, lotus, Nymphaea, and other specimens, all in pots.*

*A formal pool in which lotus and water lilies are combined, adorned by an antique Chinese stone figure.*

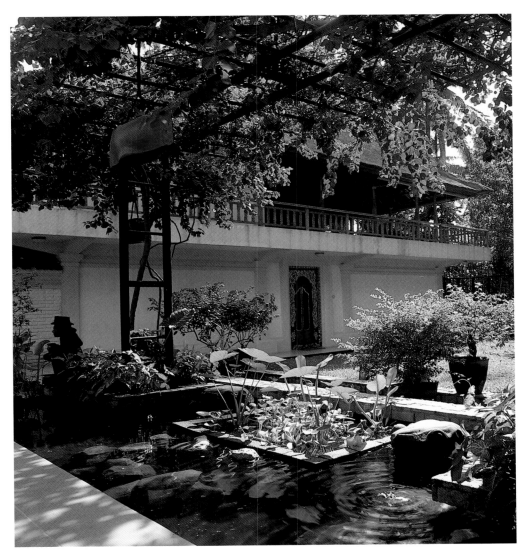

*A* pond for assorted water plants off the terrace of a house in Bali.

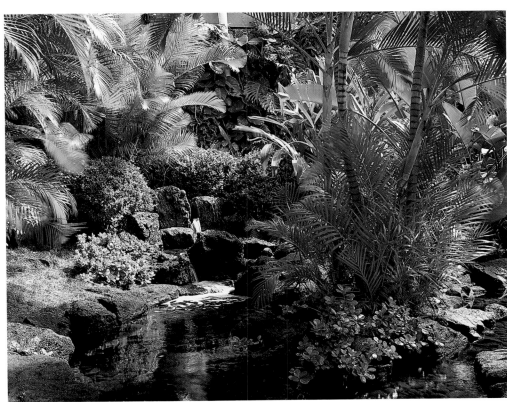

*A*n informal pool with rocks and an artificial waterfall at the Kahala Hilton Hotel.

## Swimming Pools

SERVING BOTH AS WATER FEATURES and as places for family recreation, swimming pools are incorporated into garden designs throughout the tropics. Some, especially those in hotel gardens, are of impressive size and imaginative configuration; the pool at the Amandari Hotel in Bali, for instance, follows the irregular form of rice terraces that spill dramatically into a valley far below, while others are built around luxuriantly planted little islands; even standard rectangular pools can be given an individual distinction through the use of unusual fountains or large containers planted with flowering shrubs and creepers.

*Swimming* pool *of the Amandari Hotel at Ubud in Bali.*

*Natural rocks are incorporated into the pool at the Pelangi Resort in Langkawi, Malaysia.*

*A salt-water pool in Phuket, built in the rocks overlooking the Andaman Sea.*

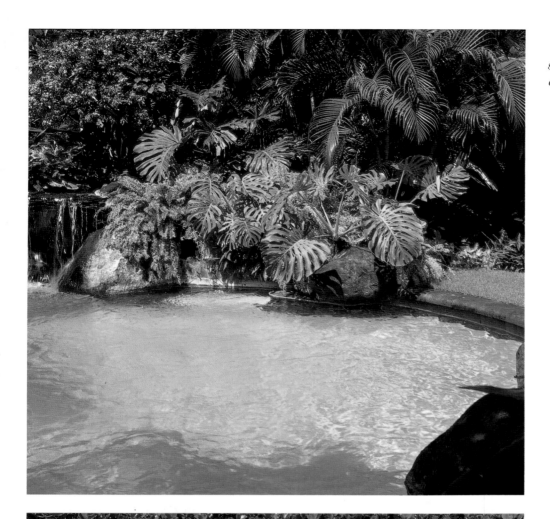

*A pool in a garden in Bali, softened by a dense tropical planting.*

*A fountain of black stone covered with small Bromeliads supplies water for a Hawaiian garden pool.*

*Opposite: a pool overlooking the Pacific Ocean in Honolulu; pink Mussaenda blooms on the left, white Plumeria on the right.*

# Bibliography

AMRANAND, PIMSAI *Gardening in Bangkok.* The Siam Society, Bangkok, 1976.

BASHAM, A.L. *The Wonder that was India.* Fontana Books, New Delhi, 1981

BRUGGEMAN, L. *Tropical Plants and Their Cultivation.* Thames and Hudson, London, 1957.

CLAY, HORACE F. and HUBBARD, JAMES C. *The Hawai'i Garden: Tropical Exotics.* University Press of Hawaii, Honolulu, 1977.

EISEMAN, FRED and MARGARET *Flowers of Bali.* Periplus Editions, Berkeley, 1988.

GILLILAND, H.B. *Common Malayan Plants.* University of Malaya Press, Kuala Lumpur, 1958.

GRAF, ALFRED BIRD *Tropica, Color Cyclopedia of Exotic Plants and Trees.* Roehrs Company, New Jersey, 1978.

GREENSILL, T.M. *Gardening in the Tropics.* Evans Brothers Ltd., London, 1964.

HARGREAVES, DOROTHY and BOB *Hawaii Blossoms.* Hargreaves Industrial, Portland, Oregon, 1958.

HEPPER, J. NIGEL (ed.) *Kew, Gardens for Science and Pleasure.* Her Majesty's Stationery Office, London, 1982.

HOLTUM, R.E. *Gardening in the Lowlands of Malaya.* Straits Times Press, Singapore, 1953.

HYAMS, EDWARD and MACQUITTY, WILLIAM *Great Botanical Gardens of the World.* Thomas Nelson and Sons, London, 1969.

JELLICOE, GEOFFREY and SUSAN (ed.) *The Oxford Companion to Gardens.* Oxford University Press, Oxford, 1986.

KUCK, LORAINE E. and TONGG, RICHARD C. *Hawaiian Flowers and Flowering Trees.* Charles E. Tuttle Company, Tokyo, 1960.

McMAKIN, PATRICK D. *A Field Guide to the Flowering Plants of Thailand.* White Lotus Co. Ltd., Bangkok, 1988.

MacMILLAN, H.F. *Tropical Planting and Gardening.* Macmillan and Company, London, 1935.

MENNINGER, EDWIN A. *Flowering Trees of the World.* Hearthside Press, New York, 1962.

MERRILL, ELMER D. *Plant Life of the Pacific World.* Charles E. Tuttle Company, Tokyo, 1981.

MOIR, MAY A. *The Garden Watcher.* Harold L. Lyon Arboretum, University of Hawaii, Honolulu, 1983.

PICKELL, DAVID (ed.) *Bali, Island of the Gods.* Periplus Editions, Inc., Berkeley, 1990.

POLUNIN, IVAN *Plants and Flowers of Singapore.* Times Editions, Singapore, 1987.

SAVAGE, VICTOR R. *Western Impressions of Nature and Landscape in Southeast Asia.* Singapore University Press, Singapore, 1984.

SCIDMORE, E.R. *Java, The Garden of the East.* Oxford University Press, Singapore, 1984.

STEINER, DR. MONA LISA *Philippine Ornamental Plants.* Carmeno and Bauermann Inc., Manila, 1960.

THOMAS, ARTHUR *Gardening in Hot Countries.* Faber and Faber, London, 1965.

TINSLEY, BONNIE *Visions of Delight: The Singapore Botanic Gardens through the Ages.* Singapore Botanic Gardens, Singapore, 1989.

WHITTLE, TYLER *The Plant Hunters.* Heinemann, London, 1970.

# Acknowledgments

This book would not have been possible without the generous assistance of many people in a variety of countries. The author and photographer wish particularly to thank the following:

Mr Putu Aryasuta of the Bali Hyatt Hotel, Mr and Mrs John Ault, Mr Joop Ave, Director General of Tourism for the Republic of Indonesia, Mrs Cobey Black, Mr Bernard Brack of the Bangkok Hilton International Hotel, Mr and Mrs Paul Cassiday, Mr Manop Charoensuk, Mrs Gerald Corbett, Ms Nancy Daniels of the Kahala Hilton Hotel, M.L.Tri Devakul, Ms Trina Dingler Ebert of Aman Resorts, Mr and Mrs John Ede of the Mandai Gardens, Ms Cheryl Engstrom of the Westin Kauai Hotel, Dr Fritz A. Frauchiger of the Contemporary Museum in Honolulu, Mrs Sue Girson, Mr Rio Helmi, Mr Brent Hesselyn, Ms Henrietta Ho of the Hyatt Hotel Group, Mr Tan Jiew Hoe, Mr and Mrs Hans Hofer, Ms Stephanie Kaluahine-Reid of the Westin Kauai Hotel, Mr Toshi Kaneko of the Allerton Gardens, Dr Tan Wee Kiat of the Singapore Botanic Gardens, Mr Sunny Khoo of the Bali Hyatt Hotel, Mr Melvin Labra, Mr Setapong Lekawatana, Mrs Gretchen Liu, Mr Leonard Lueras, Mr Islay Lyons, Dr and Mrs Thomas Macmillan, Mr Leland Miyano, Mrs May Moir, Mr Frank Morgan, Ms Linda Moriarity, Mrs Fern Pietsch, M.R. Kukrit Pramoj, Dr Yoneo Sagawa of the Lyon Arboretum, Khunying Lurasakdi Sampatisiri, Mr Victor Sassoon, Mr George Staples, Mr Jurg Suter, Mr Hiroshi Tagami, Mrs Jean Thomas, Mrs Bonnie Tinsley of the Singapore Botanical Gardens, Mrs Anne Tofield, Mr Chaiwut Tulyadhan, Mr Richard Via, Ms Marisa Viravaidhya, Mr and Mrs Yvan Van Outrive, Mr Prasart Vongsakul, Mr William Waterfall, Mr Lyndon Wester, Mr Made Wijaya (Michael White) of Pacific Landscape Design, Mr and Mrs Wiya Wawo-Runtu, Dr Keith Wooliams of the Waimea Arboretum, Ms Ploenpit Wuttayagon.

# Index

(*Page numbers in italics refer to illustrations*)